COME
AND FOLLOW

An Introduction to Christian Discipleship

F. Washington Jarvis

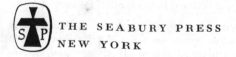

THE SEABURY PRESS
NEW YORK

In grateful memory of

MILTON SEYBERT KANAGA
Rector of Grace Church, Willoughby, Ohio,

HARRY GALLISON TREFRY
Chaplain of St. Mark's School,

and

JAMES STANLEY BEZZANT
Fellow and Dean of St. John's College, Cambridge.

"For the Lord is gracious, his mercy is everlasting; and his truth endureth from generation to generation."

All quotations from the Holy Scriptures, except where otherwise noted, are from *The New English Bible,* copyright 1961, 1970 by the Delegates of the Oxford University Press and the Syndics of the Cambridge University Press.

Other biblical quotations are from the *Revised Standard Version of the Bible,* copyrighted 1946 and 1952 by the Division of Christian Education, National Council of Churches; *The New Testament in Modern English,* copyrighted by J. B. Phillips 1958, The Macmillan Company; *The Jerusalem Bible,* copyrighted 1966, 1967, and 1968 by Darton, Longman and Todd Ltd., and Doubleday and Company, Inc.

Quotation on Polycarp's martyrdom in chapter 20 is from *A Treasury of Early Christianity,* edited by A. Fremantle (Viking, 1953).

Quotations on Luther in chapter 22 are from *Martin Luther,* E. G. Rupp and Benjamin Drewery (Edward Arnold [Publishers] Ltd., 1970).

Quotations from the Venerable Bede in chapter 23 are from *A History of the English Church and People,* translated by Leo Sherley-Price (Penguin, 1955, 1968).

Copyright © 1972 by The Seabury Press, Incorporated
Library of Congress Catalog Card Number: 73-185519
ISBN: 0-8164-2072-6
Design by Carol Basen
742-372-C-5
Printed in the United States of America

Contents

To the Reader

"Can you suggest a book that tells all about Christianity?" This often-repeated question prompted me to write *Come and Follow*. No book could possibly tell "all" about Christianity, but the time seemed ripe and the need great for a short single-volume introduction to the life of Christ and to the beliefs and practices of the Church, the company of Christ's followers.

This book arises out of seven years of teaching over 700 youths and adults in confirmation and enquirers classes and special study groups in a parish, and about 150 students in secondary school and college. These 850 have all used *Come and Follow* in preliminary forms, and I have revised it numerous times in response to their criticisms and suggestions.

This book has all the limitations of a brief introduction. It has not been possible, for example, to give much of the Old Testament background to Christ's life. I have not paused for theological debate at the many points where scholars differ in their interpretation. In chapter 8, for example, I have (in agreement with Sanders, Hunter, Barclay, et al.) discussed the six miracles in John's Gospel, whereas many scholars would say there are seven. In chapter 19 I have taken one of several possible views on the chronology of Paul's life, but have not mentioned or discussed other possibilities. Examples such as these could be multiplied many times.

Though prayer and worship are dealt with at some length, this book is not a manual of the spiritual life. And though *Come and Follow* focuses largely on what is common to all Christians, a few chapters at the end deal with the Church's history and worship from the viewpoint of one particular group of Christians, the Anglican Communion.

I have made extensive use of the New Testament accounts of Jesus, and in a real sense they are the heart of the book to which the rest is commentary. Unless otherwise indicated these passages are taken from *The New English Bible*. An index at the back shows where passages can be found both in *Come and Follow* and in the Book of Common Prayer. Prayer Book references in the text are indicated by the letters PB followed by the page number.

The list of those who have helped with this book is very long. Most of all I am grateful for the forbearance and patience of the many victims of earlier versions of this book and of my teaching—especially the people of St. Paul's Parish, Cleveland Heights, Ohio, and the students of University School. As the Psalmist truly said, "You are the blessed of the Lord, you and your children."

My debt is great to a number of individuals. From the outset Dr. Dora P. Chaplin provided great support and help. Aric Greenfield, Mrs. Meade Spencer, my sister Faith Jarvis Smith, and Alan Buchmann have read large parts of the manuscript and offered invaluable advice. Thomas Hoyt Jones II devoted the greater part of almost two months to helping me improve the first half of the book. My colleague at University School, Richard A. Hawley, offered extensive and extremely useful suggestions on almost every chapter. Lee Richard Kravitz read the entire final manuscript with extreme care and suggested many improvements. Professor Eldon J. Epp and the Rev. James L. P. Trautwein saved me from a number of blunders and drew my attention to several serious omissions. Miss Jessica Flack has patiently multilithed various predecessors to this book over the years. Finally, I am grateful beyond expression to Mrs. Nathaniel W. Baker, who has criticized and encouraged me about this book for eight years, and to Mrs. R. Wallace Hutson, who has decoded my handwriting, typed and retyped the book from start to finish, and endured the ups and downs of my feelings about it. For errors and inadequacies which remain, I am alone responsible.

F. WASHINGTON JARVIS

St. Stephen's Day, 1971

Man's Search for Meaning

Most of us find our time and energy occupied by the pressing day-to-day concerns of life—providing for our families, the obligations of a job or of education, the demands made on us by both the happy and unhappy relationships we have with those around us. From time to time, however, some external event or person or some inner urge causes us to pause in the midst of the busyness of life to ask ourselves what it all means.

Life is bewildering. Chance often appears to govern it. Some people get all the breaks, others none. By accident of birth the gates of opportunity are open to some and closed to others. Selfish and cruel persons often seem to lead full and happy lives, while generous and loving persons get nowhere in life. Virtue is not its own reward. Honesty is often not the best policy. Diseases such as cancer suddenly strike down and destroy indiscriminately. Or an automobile accident does. And the only certain thing about life is that in the end we all die.

Looking at ourselves as a species it is difficult not to be confused. Perhaps all we can say is that we're neither perfect nor immortal. The founders of every community have always found it necessary very quickly to establish a prison and a cemetery.

No sooner do we hail man's technical achievements and his skillful use of natural resources, than we suddenly become keenly aware that man has carelessly polluted rivers and

4

air and plundered and wasted resources. We pride ourselves on having created just and orderly government and international understanding, yet the bigger government gets the more unresponsive to individuals it seems to become, and men still settle differences by wars, destroying each other's families and homes. We think of ourselves as having come of age. We are educated, cultured, sophisticated. Yet no society has ever had a higher crime rate or witnessed more irrational violence. We experience unprecedented material well-being, and yet a quarter of the world starves and squalid poverty is rampant in every city of the world's richest nation. We take pride in our conquest of disease, yet the same scientific genius has given us the power to destroy all human life as we know it by pushing a button.

These are some of the raw materials we have to work with as we try to find some meaning in life. Obviously nobody has all the answers. But as thoughtful people we all seek to find a philosophy of life that creates some order out of the chaos and that offers some clue to understanding the over-all meaning of things.

There are many philosophies of life. Communism, for instance, sees man's ultimate satisfaction arising from material well-being. Man will find meaning and happiness in life, in the Communist view, when goods are distributed fairly among those who produce them. The hedonist follows the ancient Epicurean belief that pleasure in the present is what makes life meaningful: "eat, drink, and be merry, for tomorrow we die." Certain existentialist schools (of Sartre and Camus, for example) assert that life is ultimately absurd and meaningless, but that individuals can create happiness for themselves in the present by "doing their thing."

This book is about one of the many philosophies of life, Christianity, which sees in a single figure in human history what it believes are significant clues to the meaning of existence and to the discovery of happiness.

The Mystery of Life

We must begin without any illusions. Each of us is one of four billion temporary little specks on a little speck in a vast universe. We cannot fully understand the universe and its meaning and we are essentially powerless in the face of it. We are rather like ants crawling along Fifth Avenue in New York City trying to comprehend the Empire State Building. Yet, just because we cannot fully comprehend the meaning of the universe does not mean that either it or our lives are meaningless. Though we cannot fathom the mystery of life, we can have occasional glimpses into that mystery, glimpses which give us some clues about life's meaning.

A traveler once stayed five days in a valley town in the Alps. He had been told of the towering splendor of the mountains. But each morning when he went to his window, the mountains were lost in the clouds, and all he could see was the dreary little village around him. On the last day he was awakened by brilliant sunshine and went to the window to see the gleaming mountains towering above him. Then after dressing and having breakfast he emerged from his hotel again to see clouds covering the mountains, and the day grew grayer and grayer. This is, perhaps, a parable of life. In life there are many clouds—confusions and problems. But occasionally, for a brief time, the clouds disperse and we perceive the beauty and the meaning of existence. In the midst of the clouds we sometimes catch a glimpse of the mountains. In the midst of life there are moments in which we are "surprised by joy," in which we have a definite feeling or intuition of meaning and purpose.

Some can hear a Beethoven symphony and say afterward that it is just noise and makes no sense. Others, however, go away inspired, sensing structure and majesty in the same symphony. No one can prove that the symphony is beautiful or meaningful. Yet those who believe they have experienced beauty in the symphony are reluctant to accept the idea that they are deluded. Many claim that they have experienced moments of beauty and meaning in music, art, nature, and personal relationships that lifted them out of their everyday lives to perceive something real and lasting. These moments are fleeting, and the clouds return. One cannot freeze a great moment in a personal relationship; one cannot bottle a great moment in music. Yet in these brief experiences we glimpse some of the beauty and meaning of the mystery of existence.

Insights into the Mystery of Life

Every philosophy of life in every age has based itself on what men have discovered in these moments of insight. Christianity is no exception. Since Christianity is comparatively young it is built on the insights of hundreds of generations of human life which preceded it.

At the dawn of human consciousness hundreds of thousands of years ago, primitive man intuitively felt the presence of forces in the universe beyond his comprehension and control, and he instinctively felt his happiness was somehow connected with those forces. Most ancient people were polytheists; that is, they believed many gods (or forces) were at work in the universe. At first they venerated those forces of nature which were necessary for existence: the sun, the soil, the rain. They treated them as personal and addressed them with requests and flatteries and hopes.

As men matured they saw that these forces were not entirely separate but were interrelated as part of one orderly system—a universe. Polytheism gave way to monotheism, the belief that all existing things originate from and are held together by one single creative Force. "God" is the name men came to use for the origin and meaning of existence.

Christianity emerges from two groups of monotheists. Jesus and most of the early Christians were Jews, and Judaism was the most sophisticated and mature monotheistic philosophy of the ancient world. The Old Testament reveals the Jews' progressive advance toward belief in one God, and shows how that belief affected the way they lived. Eventually the Jews decided that happiness came from attuning themselves to God, insofar as they could. The other great monotheistic forerunner of Christianity is the Athenian fifth century B.C. philosophic school of Plato. Plato sought to persuade his fellow polytheistic Greeks that all existing things have their origin and coherence and meaning in a single Mind which transcends the visible passing things of earth.

The Christian view is this: God—the same God—has been there from the beginning. As man progressed he discerned more and more of the nature of God and what his purpose is for the universe and man. Like primitive man we observe the beauty and order and miracle of nature: the seasons, day following night, the regular patterns of the planets, the endless creative possibilities of the soil. We share in the philosophic monotheism of Plato (we see the universe as one—coherent and unified) and in the ethical monotheism of the Jews (we instinctively feel that there must be an ultimate purpose and justice to life).

But Christianity goes beyond its predecessors in a unique way. It asserts that at a moment in history—in a single human being—God showed men what he is like and what his purpose is. About the year 4 B.C., in a remote minor province of the Roman Empire, to a poor and unknown couple, a child was born—Jesus. Christianity finds in the life and teachings of that human being the clearest disclosure of what life is all about.

Christianity and Other Ways of Life

If you place a copy of Swift's *Gulliver's Travels* in the hands of a large group of people, each will have a different understanding of it. Children will see it as an interesting fairy tale. Certain adults will see it as a satire on human nature. Historians will see it as a commentary on the political scene of Swift's day. Yet it remains one and the same book.

So it is with men as they grope for life's meaning. They catch glimpses—some deeper than others—into the nature of reality. These differing insights may be caused by age, by background, by inclination. Primitive men understood the meaning of things at a childish level. Man's insights matured as he matured, but they still vary immensely. It is important to keep in mind, therefore, that, even though Christianity finds in Jesus the most complete revelation of God, it nevertheless respects any other religion or philosophy which honestly seeks for the meaning of life. Even though Buddhists and Hindus, for example, see God from a different viewpoint than Christians and call him by a different name, they are nevertheless seeking to know and follow the same God Christians know and follow.

No man has seen God; no man can fully understand the mystery of life. But Christians believe that in Jesus man is given as clear an indication of the meaning of life as it is possible to have. No life in all history has shown such magnetic attraction for men of every age and place. The rest of this book is an attempt to meet and discover that person who, as Albert Schweitzer wrote,

comes to us as One unknown, without a name, as of old, by the lake-side, He came to those men who knew Him not. He speaks to us the same word: "Follow thou me!" and sets us to the tasks which He has to fulfill for our time. He commands. And to those who obey Him, whether they be wise or simple, He will reveal Himself in the toils, the conflicts, the suffering which they shall pass through in His fellowship and, as an ineffable mystery, they shall learn in their own experience who He is.

The Incarnation 2

In the following chapters we shall explore some of the things Jesus did and said in the brief thirty-odd years of his life. We shall be looking at documents which were all written by biased people. All the information we have about Jesus comes from men who had known him and who were absolutely convinced that in him they had seen what God is like and what human life is all about.

The early Christians shared the experience of Christ and their lives had been transformed. They were confused about how to explain what they felt about Jesus in terms others would understand, and they all used different words and philosophical terms when they tried to explain. We may compare the early Christians in their exuberance with a man who has fallen in love. He knows he's madly in love—he is captivated by the person with whom he's in love. But he has difficulty in explaining to others what it is he "sees in her." He may use ecstatic terms: "She's fantastic!" "She's incredible." He may describe certain of her physical features. He may go deeper and try to describe non-physical features: her "tenderness," her "understanding." But all these terms are utterly inadequate in describing the whole experience he has of her.

So it was with the early Christians. Their lives had been transformed by an experience, but they were left groping for words to describe it. They expressed their convictions about Jesus in a variety of ways. We are going to look at only two of those ways: that of Paul, the earliest Christian writer, and that of John, one of the last biblical writers.

Paul's Attempt to Explain Jesus' Significance

Paul's encounter with Jesus on the Damascus Road (see chapter 19) changed him from a persecutor of Christians into Christianity's greatest leader. When Paul set about to explain what it was about Jesus that was so significant, he said that Jesus was God himself, laying aside for a time all his divine attributes, limiting and humbling himself to live among men as a man. Jesus was God incarnate, God in the flesh.

Let Christ Jesus be your example as to what your attitude should be. For he, who has always been God by nature, did not cling to his prerogatives as God's equal, but stripped himself of all privileges by consenting to be a slave by nature and being born as mortal man. And, having become man, he humbled himself by living a life of utter obedience even to the extent of dying, *and the death he died was the death of a common criminal.* That is why God has now lifted him so high, and has given him the name beyond all names, so that at the name of Jesus "every knee shall bow", whether in Heaven or earth or under the earth. And that is why, in the end, "every tongue shall confess" that Jesus Christ is the Lord, to the glory of God the Father.   PHILIPPIANS 2:5-11, PHILLIPS

In contemporary terms this would be like an affluent suburbanite giving up the securities of his life (his family, job, and connections) and going to live in the slums, to share the life of the disadvantaged and to understand and help them. Recently the newspapers reported the complaint of a slum-dweller that in the previous year a number of different government and social workers had come to his house making surveys and asking him questions about slum conditions. He is reported to have remarked: "If they really want to know what life's like down here, if they really care about helping us, why don't they come down here to live? They'll soon

find out." Paul points out that when God became a man, he
became one of us completely. He was born, he was tempted,
he hungered, thirsted, was tired, knew great joy and success,
experienced sadness and despair, had friends yet also was
lonely, suffered, and finally died.

John's Attempt to Explain Jesus' Significance

John, writing later, tries to speak of Jesus' significance in
a somewhat wider context. He views Jesus as the culmination
of God's disclosure of himself. John speaks of God's revelation of himself as God's *word.* Our own words reveal much
of our inner selves to others. So God has been "speaking" his
word to us since the creation of the world.

At the beginning God expressed himself. That personal expression, that word, was with God and was God, and he existed
with God from the beginning.

Just as our words *are* us (in that they express us) to others,
so God's word, his expression of himself in the creation of the
world, *is* God, in that it expresses God to us.

All creation took place through him [the word], and none took
place without him. All that came to be was alive with his life,
and that life was the light of men.

All creation radiated God's presence, and the more deeply
men perceived the radiance of God's presence in creation
the more enlightened they were about the meaning of life.
No matter how few perceived that light, no matter how many
turned their backs on it, it was never extinguished.

The light still shines in the darkness, and the darkness has
never put it out.

Finally, after thousands of years in which men but dimly perceived God, after centuries of hope and expectation of a clearer understanding of God, John the Baptist appeared in the wilderness to announce that God was about to express himself more clearly.

A man called John was sent by God as a witness to the light. This man was not himself the light; he was sent simply as a personal witness to that light. The real light which enlightens every man was even then coming into the world.

God expressed himself in a man—Jesus Christ. Though in Christ God spoke to the very world which he had been expressing himself to since creation, God's expression of himself in Christ went largely unrecognized. It was as a symphony played to predominantly tone-deaf listeners.

He came into the world—the world he had created; but the world, though it owed its being to him, did not recognize him. He came into his own creation, and his own people would not accept him.

Yet those who were quiet enough to hear God's expression of himself, those who patiently and humbly sought to understand his disclosure, were able to perceive him.

But to all who did receive him, to those who have yielded him their allegiance, he gave the right to become children of God. These were the men who truly believed in him, and their birth depended not on the course of nature nor on any impulse or plán of man, but on God.

To perceive God's word, to live by this new light shed on life in Christ, was to be reborn to a new way of life in which men could gradually become God's children.

Christ then is the completion of God's long revelation of himself. In Christ, God spoke to men in a human being, pitched his tent among men as a man. This event is known as the Incarnation—God becoming man.

So the word of God became a human being and lived among us. We saw his splendour (the splendour of a father's only son), full of grace and truth.

Christ is God's full expression of himself in human terms. To those who hear God's word and see his light a whole new way of life opens up:

Every one of us has shared in his riches—there is a grace in our lives because of his grace. For while the Law was given by Moses, grace and truth came through Jesus Christ.

In his concluding statement John uses another term to describe Christ: *Son.* He says Jesus shows what God is like, just as a son who is intimate with his father shows what his father is like:

It is true that no one has ever seen God at any time. Yet the divine and only Son, who lives in closest intimacy with the Father, has made him known.

JOHN 1:1-14, 16-18
PHILLIPS and NEB interwoven

A Modern Parable

Jesus often used parables to explain things to his followers. Perhaps this modern parable may be helpful in our discussion of the Incarnation.

It had been snowing for twenty-four hours. Knowing that it had been a hard winter, I filled the bird feeder with an extra supply of feed that morning. Since the feeder was sheltered, it held the only food not hidden by the snow. A short while later a small bird appeared in the yard, obviously weak, hungry, and cold. Searching for food, he pecked at the snow. How helpless I felt! I wanted to go out and point to the feeder, but had I opened the door to throw out more food, he would have flown away.

Then I realized that only if I were another bird could I indicate to him where he could find food. Only if I were another bird could I fly with him, identify myself with his hunger and cold, and let him know that I understood and cared.

Our God, looking at man, knew that he must become one of us in order that we might understand his language; in order that we might know his love for us; in order that we might know his forgiveness; in order that we might point above our heads to the source of nourishment and eternal life. The Word, his Word, became flesh! God was in Christ, reconciling the words to himself.   BETTY E. STONE, *Lenten Devotions*

Why the Incarnation?

We may not understand exactly *how* Jesus was born or how it is possible for God to become a man. But John tells us something of the *why* of the Incarnation. Unlike many of the philosophies and religions in which men seek God, Christianity asserts that God enters the world as a man to seek men, to call them into relationship with him as his sons.

God loved the world so much that he gave his only Son, that everyone who has faith in him may not die but have eternal life. It was not to judge the world that God sent his Son into the world, but that through him the world might be saved. The man who puts his faith in him does not come under judgment; but the unbeliever has already been judged in that he has not given his allegiance to God's only Son. Here lies the test; the light has come into the world, but men preferred darkness to light because their deeds were evil. Bad men all hate the light and avoid it, for fear their practices should be shown up. The honest man comes to the light so that it may be clearly seen that God is in all he does.   JOHN 3:16-21

Jesus is the light that has come into the world in that he shows what man can be if man accepts God's love and chooses to be God's own child.

He was in the world; but the world, though it owed its being to him, did not recognize him. He entered his own realm, and his own would not receive him. But to all who did receive him, to those who have yielded him their allegiance, he gave the right to become children of God, not born of any human stock, or by the fleshly desire of a human father, but the offspring of God himself.   JOHN 1:10-13

Our human calling is nothing less than to become sons of God, to be lifted up out of our little lives into something greater, more beautiful, and more lasting. Not only is Jesus God's expression of himself, but he shows us, as no other human before or since, how rich and full human life can be could we but realize and accept our calling as sons of God. Perhaps this is what St. Athanasius meant when he said, "God became man that we might become divine," and what St. Ireneus had in mind when he said "God became what we are to make us what he is."

Only two of the four Gospels (Matthew and Luke) record any details about the birth of Jesus. Both see in the events of his human birth the clear action of God at work.

Matthew's Account

No book has a more boring beginning than the New Testament. It opens with Matthew's tracing of the ancestors of Joseph, "the husband of Mary, who gave birth to Jesus." Matthew was a Jew who shared his people's expectation of the Messiah—the coming of God to reign on earth. Jewish tradition stated that the Messiah would be a descendant of King David. Matthew is concerned to show that, through Joseph his father, Jesus is the descendant of David and many of the other great figures of Israel's past.

A table of the descent of Jesus Christ, son of David, son of Abraham. Abraham was the father of Isaac, Isaac of Jacob, Jacob of Judah and his brothers, Judah of Perez and Zarah (their mother was Tamar), Perez of Hezron, Hezron of Ram, Ram of Amminadab, Amminadab of Nahshon, Nahshon of Salma, Salma of Boaz (his mother was Rahab), Boaz of Obed (his mother was Ruth), Obed of Jesse; and Jesse was the father of King David. David was the father of Solomon (his mother had been the wife of Uriah), Solomon of Rehoboam, Rehoboam of Abijah, Abijah of Asa, Asa of Jehoshaphat, Jehoshaphat of Joram, Joram of Azariah, Azariah of Jotham, Jotham of Ahaz, Ahaz of Hezekiah, Hezekiah of Manasseh, Manasseh of Amon, Amon of Josiah; and Josiah was the father of Jeconiah and his brothers at the time of the deportation to Babylon. After the deporta-

tion Jeconiah was the father of Shealtiel, Shealtiel of Zerubbabel, Zerubbabel of Abiud, Abiud of Eliakim, Eliakim of Azor,
Azor of Zadok, Zadok of Achim, Achim of Eliud, Eliud of Eleazar, Eleazar of Matthan, Matthan of Jacob, Jacob of Joseph, the
husband of Mary, who gave birth to Jesus called Messiah.

MATTHEW 1:1-16

Some of the people mentioned above are illustrious. Others
are not: Tamar was incestuous, Rahab was a whore, Ruth
was a foreigner, and Solomon's mother (Bathsheba) was an
adulteress and assisted her lover in murdering her husband.
Matthew's genealogy, then, identifies Jesus with humanity
at its worst as well as at its best. Matthew wishes us to see
that Jesus is firmly rooted in the human race with all its
potential for evil as well as for good.

But Matthew is also certain that in this human birth something of cosmic consequence is taking place. A strain of Jewish prophecy anticipated that the Messiah would be born of
a virgin. Matthew shared this expectation. Since Matthew
believed that Jesus was the Messiah, he therefore infers that
the birth of Jesus must have taken place in this special way,
and that God himself (not Joseph) was the father of Jesus:

This is the story of the birth of the Messiah. Mary his mother
was betrothed to Joseph; before their marriage she found that
she was with child by the Holy Spirit. Being a man of principle,
and at the same time wanting to save her from exposure,
Joseph desired to have the marriage contract set aside quietly.
He had resolved on this, when an angel of the Lord appeared
to him in a dream. 'Joseph son of David,' said the angel, 'do
not be afraid to take Mary home with you as your wife. It is
by the Holy Spirit that she has conceived this child. She will
bear a son; and you shall give him the name Jesus (Saviour),
for he will save the people from their sins.' All this happened
in order to fulfil what the Lord declared through the prophet:
'The virgin will conceive and bear a son, and he shall be called
Emmanuel', a name which means 'God is with us'. Rising from

sleep Joseph did as the angel had directed him; he took Mary
home to be his wife, but had no intercourse with her until her
son was born. And he named the child Jesus.

MATTHEW 1:18-25

Luke's Account

Luke, though he in no way contradicts Matthew, selects
an entirely different group of incidents upon which to base
his account of Jesus' birth. Yet, like Matthew, Luke finds a
divine significance in the events he recounts. In trying to
convey the significance of these events, Luke often turns to
poetic and symbolic language. His account begins with the
Annunciation to Mary.

In the sixth month the angel Gabriel was sent from God to a
town in Galilee called Nazareth, with a message for a girl betrothed to a man named Joseph, a descendant of David; the
girl's name was Mary. The angel went in and said to her, 'Greetings, most favoured one! The Lord is with you.' But she was
deeply troubled by what he said and wondered what this greeting might mean. Then the angel said to her, 'Do not be afraid,
Mary, for God has been gracious to you; you shall conceive
and bear a son, and you shall give him the name Jesus. He will
be great; he will bear the title "Son of the Most High"; the
Lord God will give him the throne of his ancestor David, and
he will be king over Israel for ever; his reign shall never end.'

LUKE 1:26-33

Let us pause here to consider briefly the subject of angels.
The word "angel" in Greek means "messenger." Note that
the angel above (as other angels in the New Testament) is
not described as having wings or halo or wearing a white
robe. In fact he is not described at all. Men have always
speculated on how God conveys himself to man—how the gap
between the purely spiritual and the earthly is bridged. God
obviously must disclose himself in terms man can under-

stand. To primitive man God was perceived in thunder and
rain and clouds. The Jews expected God to communicate
with men by means of divine messengers. It is no accident
that the angel who appeared to Joan of Arc in the Middle
Ages looked exactly like the angel in the stainedglass window of her parish church. We today do not expect God to
communicate with us by means of angels. We have our own
expectations; we use a different mythology: "I had a brain
storm," "it suddenly came to me," "my intuition told me."
But to an age which expected God to speak to man by means
of divine messengers, that is how God would communicate
himself.

Luke next tells us that while Mary was pregnant she went
to visit her cousin Elizabeth, wife of Zechariah. Elizabeth
also was pregnant with the child who was later to become
known as John the Baptizer.

About this time Mary set out and went straight to a town in
the uplands of Judah. She went into Zechariah's house and
greeted Elizabeth. And when Elizabeth heard Mary's greeting,
the baby stirred in her womb. Then Elizabeth was filled with
the Holy Spirit and cried aloud. 'God's blessing is on you above
all women, and his blessing is on the fruit of your womb.'

                                                    LUKE 1:39-42

Filled with joy at the impending birth, Mary shares her
gladness with Elizabeth, and, in words parallel to Scripture,
pours out both her gratitude and her hopes. Her words are
called the *Magnificat* (from the Latin) and still today are
used by Christians as a hymn (see Prayer Book, page 26).

And Mary said: 'Tell out, my soul, the greatness of the Lord,
rejoice, rejoice, my spirit, in God my saviour; so tenderly has
he looked upon his servant, humble as she is. For from this day
forth, all generations will count me blessed, so wonderfully has

he dealt with me, the Lord, the Mighty One. His name is Holy; his mercy sure from generation to generation toward those who fear him; the deeds his own right arm has done disclose his might: the arrogant of heart and mind he has put to rout, he has brought down monarchs from their thrones, but the humble have been lifted high. The hungry he has satisfied with good things, the rich sent empty away. He has ranged himself at the side of Israel his servant; firm in his promise to our forefathers, he has not forgotten to show mercy to Abraham and his children's children, for ever.'   LUKE 1:46-55

Her joy in anticipation of giving birth to a child is coupled with a sense of indignation at the injustices and evils of the world into which the child will be born. The *Magnificat* has been called more revolutionary than the Communist Manifesto. It anticipates with hope a revolution which will restore justice and brotherhood to the world.

Luke next describes the conditions surrounding Jesus' birth. Probably no child born into the world that day seemed to have poorer prospects. God came among men not in power, force, and splendor, but in weakness, poverty, and quietness. The account of Jesus' birth has been called history's greatest paradox: the Saviour of the world, born in a minor province to poor parents in a stable far away from home.

In those days a decree was issued by the Emperor Augustus for a registration to be made throughout the Roman world. This was the first registration of its kind; it took place when Quirinius was governor of Syria. For this purpose everyone made his way to his own town; and so Joseph went up to Judaea from the town of Nazareth in Galilee, to be registered at the city of David, called Bethlehem, because he was of the house of David by descent; and with him went Mary who was betrothed to him. She was expecting a child, and while they

were there the time came for her baby to be born, and she
gave birth to a son, her first-born. She wrapped him in his
swaddling clothes, and laid him in a manger, because there
was no room for them to lodge in the house.   LUKE 2:1-7

But, like Matthew, Luke sets side by side with Jesus' humanity (his humble birth) his conviction that in Jesus' birth
God's divine activity can be perceived. Luke brings this out
in his account of the vision of the shepherds, their certainty
that this child is the long-awaited coming of God to earth.

Now in this same district there were shepherds out in the
fields, keeping watch through the night over their flock, when
suddenly there stood before them an angel of the Lord, and
the splendour of the Lord shone round them. They were terror-
stricken, but the angel said, 'Do not be afraid; I have good
news for you: there is great joy coming to the whole people.
Today in the city of David a deliverer has been born to you—
the Messiah, the Lord. And this is your sign: you will find a
baby lying wrapped in his swaddling clothes, in a manger.' All
at once there was with the angel a great company of the
heavenly host, singing the praises of God:

'Glory to God in highest heaven.
And on earth his peace for men on whom his favour rests.'

After the angels had left them and gone into heaven the shepherds said to one another, 'Come, we must go straight to
Bethlehem and see this thing that has happened, which the
Lord has made known to us.' So they went with all speed and
found their way to Mary and Joseph; and the baby was lying
in the manger. When they saw him, they recounted what they
had been told about this child; and all who heard were astonished at what the shepherds said. But Mary treasured up all
these things and pondered over them. Meanwhile the shepherds returned glorifying and praising God for what they had
heard and seen; it had all happened as they had been told.
                                                      LUKE 2:8-20

It was customary for minstrels to gather and sing at the birth of a Jewish child, and some scholars regard this story as a mythical elaboration on that custom. Luke's reason for including the story is clearly not just to record literal and customary events. Shepherds were the lowest class in Jewish society because they could not be at home to perform all the intricate rituals called for in the law. While respectable people slept, the shepherds had a vision of who Jesus was. Right in the event of his birth Luke sees foreshadowed Jesus' rejection by the great and his acceptance by the humble.

The Virgin Birth

Matthew and Luke, the two writers who tell us anything about Jesus' birth, both show God breaking into human existence in the birth of Jesus. Though the important thing, of course, is the fact *that* Jesus was born and not *how,* many people have worried a great deal about *how.* Below are the arguments for and against the virgin birth. You can make up your own mind.

A. Arguments in favor of the virgin birth:
　　1. Matthew clearly says Jesus was born of a virgin. Knowing Matthew's account, some interpret Luke 1:34-35 (Mary's seeming surprised joy that she will be given a child by God's Spirit) as supporting Matthew's view.
　　2. Since, in Jesus, God came into the world in the form of a human being, it is likely that Jesus' birth was accompanied by some obvious sign that it was a divine event.

B. Arguments against the virgin birth:
　　1. Matthew is alone in saying anything about a virgin birth. Reading Luke's account without knowledge of Matthew's theory of the virgin birth, we would find there only a woman's glad thankfulness to God for the assurance that she will someday be a mother.

2. Even in Matthew, Mary, who is the only one who would know for certain, never testifies how the conception took place. In fact, Mary says: "*Your father* and I have been searching for you . . ." (Luke 2:48).
3. Matthew and Luke both trace Jesus' ancestry by way of Joseph, not Mary (Matthew 1:1-17 and Luke 3:23-38). This is strange if Joseph is not the real father. Luke 2:27 and 2:43 refer to the "parents of Jesus." And in several places (for example, Matthew 13:55, Luke 4:22, and John 6:42) references made to Joseph as Jesus' father are not commented on or corrected by the Gospel writers.
4. Mark and Paul, the earliest writers, make no mention of how the birth took place.
5. Jesus nowhere requires his followers to believe any special theory about how his birth took place.
6. Matthew was a Jew. A number of Jewish prophecies anticipated the virgin birth of the Messiah, and it would have been natural for Matthew to *assume*, therefore, that Jesus (who he believed was the Messiah) was born of a virgin.
7. Since so little evidence indicates a virgin birth, and so much evidence seems to contradict it, it is logical to assume the birth was normal.

C. Some considerations:
1. The important thing is *that* God became a man, not the *manner* in which this took place.
2. If Jesus was born of a virgin, it does not prove anything about him (such as, for example, his divinity). If you discovered your next door neighbor had been born of a virgin, you would not leap to the conclusion that he was divine. If the virgin birth occurred it is a phenomenon, but nature has many phenomena.

The Years of   4
Preparation

We know almost nothing about Jesus between the time of his birth and his baptism when he was about thirty. The early Christian writers simply were not interested in Jesus' childhood. Matthew and Luke, who are not among the earliest Christian writers, wrote their accounts more than thirty-five years after Jesus' death. They are the only ones who give us any information about Jesus' early years, and even they do not tell us much.

Jesus' Childhood

Bethlehem, the birthplace of Jesus, is in Judea, which at this time was a small Jewish province of the Roman Empire. The puppet king Herod, a Jew, governed the area under Roman supervision. Astrologers, following a star, came to Judea seeking a child "born to be king of the Jews." We know little about these astrologers except that they were non-Jews from the more scientifically advanced east. Their gifts and the cost of their long journey indicate that they were men of great means, and legend has it that they were kings of minor eastern states.

Not long after his birth there arrived from the east a party of astrologers making for Jerusalem and inquiring as they went: "Where is the child born to be king of the Jews? For we saw his star in the east and we have come here to pay homage to him."

25

When King Herod heard about this he was deeply perturbed, as indeed were all the other people living in Jerusalem. So he summoned all the Jewish scribes and chief priests together and asked them where "Christ" should be born. Their reply was: "In Bethlehem, in Judaea, for this is what the prophet wrote about the matter—

> And thou Bethlehem, land of Judah,
> Art in no wise least among the princes of Judah:
> For out of thee shall come forth a governor,
> Which shall be shepherd of my people Israel."

Then Herod invited the wise men to meet him privately and found out from them the exact time when the star appeared. Then he sent them off to Bethlehem, saying: "When you get there, search for this little child with the utmost care. And when you have found him, come back and tell me—so that I may go and worship him too."

The wise men listened to the king and then went on their way to Bethlehem. And now the star, which they had seen in the east, went in front of them as they traveled until at last it shone immediately above the place where the little child lay. The sight of the star filled them with indescribable joy.

So they went into the house and saw the little child with his mother Mary. And they fell on their knees and worshiped him. Then they opened their treasures and presented him with gifts —gold, incense and myrrh. Then, since they were warned in a dream not to return to Herod, they went back to their own country by a different route.   MATTHEW 2:2-12, PHILLIPS

Some maintain that this story is a myth. Indeed, Matthew may have been speaking symbolically. The astrologers effectively represent the non-Jewish world paying homage to the long-expected Jewish child, the wisest and most educated minds discovering him who will later be called "the way, the truth, and the life," and the great and wealthy recognizing in the baby one whose being and power vastly exceeded their own. Similarly, the star which lead the astrologers may have been an element of wonder added to the story to symbolize all nature pointing to him who is later called "the light of the world."

However, the story may also be literally true. Since the stars move in regular and predictable patterns, ancient scholars attached great significance to the irregular movement of stars, regarding it as heralding a special disclosure by God. Ancient historians tell us that there was in the east at this time an almost feverish expectation of just such a divine disclosure and that many eastern potentates made pilgrimages such as the one described in this story. Astronomers also tell us that Halley's comet fell about this time and that there was a rare conjunction of Saturn and Jupiter, both of which could have created the effect of a very bright star.

Eight days after his birth, in accordance with Jewish custom, Jesus was circumcised, named, and presented in the temple. His parents' gift to the temple was that which was required of poor parents by the law.

Then, after their purification had been completed in accordance with the Law of Moses, they brought him up to Jerusalem to present him to the Lord (as prescribed in the law of the Lord: 'Every first-born male shall be deemed to belong to the Lord'), and also to make the offering as stated in the law: 'A pair of turtle doves or two young pigeons.'   LUKE 2:22-24

In the temple a devout old man, Simeon, was overcome by joy upon witnessing the newborn baby. Luke sees Simeon as an example of Judaism at its best, recognizing and accepting the long-awaited Messiah.

There was at that time in Jerusalem a man called Simeon. This man was upright and devout, one who watched and waited for the restoration of Israel, and the Holy Spirit was upon him. It had been disclosed to him by the Holy Spirit that he would not see death until he had seen the Lord's Messiah. Guided by the Spirit he came into the temple; and when the parents brought in the child Jesus to do for him what was customary under the Law, he took him in his arms, praised God, and said:

'This day, Master, thou givest thy servant his discharge in peace; now thy promise is fulfilled. For I have seen with my own eyes the deliverance which thou hast made ready in full view of all the nations: a light that will be a revelation to the heathen, and glory to thy people Israel.'   LUKE 2:25-32

Simeon's words, called the *Nunc dimittis* (from the Latin), are still used as a Christian hymn (PB, 28).

In the meantime Herod grew more and more upset by the idea of the birth of a child "born to be King of the Jews." Obsessed with fear that someone would usurp his power, he ordered all the children of Bethlehem under two years old put to death. But Joseph and Mary took the child and fled from the province, as refugees, to Egypt.

An angel of the Lord appeared to Joseph in a dream and said to him, 'Rise up, take the child and his mother and escape with them to Egypt, and stay there until I tell you; for Herod is going to search for the child to do away with him.' So Joseph rose from sleep, and taking mother and child by night he went away with them to Egypt, and there he stayed till Herod's death.   MATTHEW 2:13-14

A few months later, however, Herod died, an event which caused unrestrained celebration by the populace. Mary and Joseph were now able to return to their home town of Nazareth in Galilee, north of Bethlehem. We know almost nothing of Jesus' boyhood there. The Gospels record only one incident between the time the family returned to Nazareth and Jesus' baptism at the age of thirty. (This event, a journey to the temple to celebrate a holiday, took place when he was twelve, and is discussed in chapter 27.) We know Joseph was a carpenter and that there were other children in the family. Our imaginations lead us to picture a large family and to envision Jesus helping Joseph in the carpenter's shop. For these hidden years we must be content with Luke's summary: "As Jesus continued to grow in body and mind, he grew also in the love of God and of those who knew him."

The Baptism

In about A.D. 28 a strange and forbidding figure appears in the desert near the Dead Sea: John the Baptizer. John is an uncompromising and extreme personality: he dresses roughly, he eats only enough to live, and he warns men that there is an ultimate justice to life, and that in the end those who choose evil will be harshly judged.

John the Baptist appeared as a preacher in the Judaean wilderness; his theme was: 'Repent; for the kingdom of Heaven is upon you!' It is of him that the prophet Isaiah spoke when he said, 'A voice crying aloud in the wilderness, "Prepare a way for the Lord; clear a straight path for him." '

John's clothing was a rough coat of camel's hair, with a leather belt round his waist, and his food was locusts and wild honey. They flocked to him from Jerusalem, from all Judaea, and the whole Jordan valley, and were baptized by him in the River Jordan, confessing their sins.

When he saw many of the Pharisees and Sadducees coming for baptism he said to them: 'You vipers' brood! Who warned you to escape from the coming retribution? Then prove your repentance by the fruit it bears; and do not presume to say to yourselves, "We have Abraham for our father." I tell you that God can make children for Abraham out of these stones here. Already the axe is laid to the roots of the trees; and every tree that fails to produce good fruit is cut down and thrown on the fire. I baptize you with water, for repentance; but the one who comes after me is mightier than I. I am not fit to take off his shoes. He will baptize you with the Holy Spirit and with fire. His shovel is ready in his hand and he will winnow his thresh-ing-floor; the wheat he will gather into his granary, but he will burn the chaff on a fire that can never go out.'

MATTHEW 3:1-12

Repent means "turn around." Baptism means "washing" or "cleansing." John uses unmistakable metaphors of judgment: the chaff (those who are evil) will be separated and burned. The tree (man) not bearing good fruit will be axed. Natu-rally the respectable people were deeply threatened by John's harsh, negative warning. They thought being Abraham's children was a privilege (God was on their side); John told them it was a responsibility and warned them of the conse-quences of irresponsibility.

Then comes one to be baptized who somehow stands out from the crowd: Jesus. Identifying himself with those who come to John seeking a washing away of the old life and the construction of a new life, Jesus insists that John baptize him. John senses about Jesus an unusual serenity and good-ness, and hesitates to baptize him.

Then Jesus arrived at the Jordan from Galilee, and came to John to be baptized by him. John tried to dissuade him. 'Do you come to me?' he said; 'I need rather to be baptized by you.' Jesus replied, 'Let it be so for the present; we do well to conform in this way with all that God requires.' John then allowed him to come. After baptism Jesus came up out of the water at once, and at that moment heaven opened; he saw the Spirit of God descending like a dove to alight upon him; and a voice from heaven was heard saying, 'This is my Son, my Be-loved, on whom my favour rests.'   MATTHEW 3:13-17

Identifying himself with mankind, Jesus accepts John's cleansing, and in a flash realizes what he is to do with his life. The Spirit of God comes upon him "like a dove." So certain does he feel of his calling to be God's son that all the heavens seem to proclaim it to him. Most of us have had "mountaintop experiences," moments of insight and vision so overwhelming that words are inadequate to describe them. We find ourselves using literal picture-words: "I was swept off my feet," or "I was overwhelmed." This account of the baptism shows that Jesus used such terms when he later described to his disciples the significance of his baptism. What had been a deepening awareness over the years, Jesus now explicitly realized at his baptism. Now the private years of preparation are over and Jesus gives his life to God.

The Temptations

After this great realization of the purpose and goal of his life, Jesus goes into solitude to consider the implications of his calling. Man no sooner makes lofty resolutions than he is tempted to break them. As other men, Jesus is tempted to shirk the calling to the highest and best, and to follow an easier and more agreeable course. Alone in the desert, which symbolizes the spiritual wilderness all men must at times face, he is tested. Jesus is tempted by the devil. The devil is evil personified. The Jews realistically thought of evil as a person, because they realized that the greatest evil is personal. He is first tempted to try to attract men to him by material means rather than by spirtual means. There were great economic needs which any compassionate person would desire to satisfy, and yet Jesus knew that men's hunger was not only physical but spiritual. He overcame the temptation to lure men by bribes, and set out to win their free acceptance of him.

Jesus was then led away by the Spirit into the wilderness, to be tempted by the devil. For forty days and nights he fasted, and at the end of them he was famished. The tempter approached him and said, 'If you are the Son of God, tell these

stones to become bread.' Jesus answered, 'Scripture says,
"Man cannot live on bread alone; he lives on every word God
utters." '   MATTHEW 4:1-4

②   Secondly, Jesus is tempted to attract people to him by
sensational stunts, to impress them by spectacular acts. He is
tempted to lure people to him by catching their attention, in
the hope that once he has their attention he can do something with them. In the end, though, he refused to compromise. He wished men to choose him freely.

The devil took him to the Holy City and set him on the
parapet of the temple. 'If you are the Son of God,' he said,
'throw yourself down; for Scripture says, "He will put his
angels in charge of you, and they will support you in their arms,
for fear you should strike your foot against a stone." ' Jesus
answered him, 'Scripture says again, "You are not to put the
Lord your God to the test." '   MATTHEW 4:5-7

③   Thirdly, he is tempted to seek earthly power and popularity. The Jews hoped for a military or political hero who
would lead them in banishing the Romans from their country. But again Jesus refused to gain men's allegiance by force
or power. He refused to compromise with the devil, but
sought men's free response.

Once again, the devil took him to a very high mountain, and
showed him all the kingdoms of the world in their glory. 'All
these', he said 'I will give you, if you will only fall down and
do me homage.' But Jesus said, 'Begone, Satan! Scripture says,
"You shall do homage to the Lord your God and worship him
alone." '   MATTHEW 4:8-10

So, having come to the end of his temptations, the devil
departed, biding his time.   LUKE 4:13

Many people picture Jesus as different from us, as a person
who never felt any urge to be egocentric or selfish. The ac-

counts of Jesus' temptations, however, contradict such a portrait. Undoubtedly Jesus revealed his own agonizing temptations to his disciples to help them deal with theirs. And indications are that Jesus faced constant temptation: the devil departs from him only for a time, waiting for opportunity to tempt him again. The unknown author of A Letter to Hebrews concludes that Jesus is not "unable to sympathize with our weaknesses, but one who, because of his likeness to us, has been tested every way, only without sin." (Hebrews 4:15).

The Sermon on the Mount–1

5

After the Temptation, Jesus emerged as a public figure. As he travelled from town to town people flocked to hear him. His life and teaching seemed to radiate a whole new spirit of possibility and hope.

Jesus' exact words were not written down because writing materials in the ancient world were costly and difficult to obtain. But Jesus, like every great teacher, undoubtedly repeated certain themes and illustrations, and a large number of his teachings became firmly planted in the minds of his followers. Some thirty or forty years after Jesus' death, Matthew gathered together some of the best-known sayings of Jesus into a single document which we call The Sermon on the Mount. Matthew sees Jesus as the fulfillment of all the hopes and longings of Judaism. He pictures Jesus proclaiming a new law of love to his disciples on a hillside, as Moses had proclaimed the old law on Mount Sinai. And Matthew views the "beatitudes" as the new commandments.

The beatitudes describe what it is that makes men blessed or happy. In the beatitudes Jesus asserts as his fundamental premise that true happiness comes only from loving. Jesus has in mind a special kind of love. Our English word "love" translates several Greek words: *philia*, the love between friends or brothers; *eros*, sensual physical attraction and desire; *agape*, willed concern for someone you would not necessarily care about. The kind of love Jesus speaks about is *agape*. Agape is caring about a person because he is human.

It is sometimes caring about a person you don't know or that you don't like. Jesus urges us to "love our neighbor," even if we don't know him, and even to love our enemies. Most of us assume that happiness comes from being loved and from getting things. Jesus, strangely, tells us that happiness comes from loving and giving.

The Beatitudes	Explanation of the Beatitudes
How blest are those who know their need of God; the kingdom of heaven is theirs.	*Those who know their need of God,* who are not arrogant, who know their inadequacies.
How blest are the sorrowful; they shall find consolation.	*The sorrowful* are those who are saddened and pained by the evils and injustices of the world, and who seek to share the burdens of others.
How blest are those of a gentle spirit; they shall have the earth for their possession.	*Those of a gentle spirit* are not the defenseless victims of society or the weak-kneed; they are those whose lives are not self-assertive, but rather self-sacrificing and self-controlled.
How blest are those who hunger and thirst to see right prevail; they shall be satisfied.	*Those who are intensely concerned* to do something about the injustice, prejudice, corruption, and poverty of the world they live in.
How blest are those who show mercy; mercy shall be shown to them.	*The merciful:* those who are tolerant, patient, helpful, who do not take advantage.

How blest are those whose
hearts are pure; they shall
see God.

Those whose hearts are pure:
who are sincere, whose
single motive, in every aspect
of life, is agape.

How blest are the peace-
makers; God shall call them
his sons.

The peacemakers: those who
work to bring together and
unite men of all races
and nations.

How blest are those who
have suffered persecution for
the cause of right; the
kingdom of heaven is theirs.

*Those who stand for what is
right* no matter what the
cost in popularity, prestige,
or money.

How blest you are, when you
suffer insults and persecution
and every kind of calumny
for my sake.

Those who continue to stand
calmly for the right, who
do not grow bitter and
disillusioned.

Accept it with gladness and
exultation, for you have a
rich reward in heaven; in the
same way they persecuted
the prophets before you.
                    MATTHEW 5:3-12

The joyful calm of those who
accept the sacrifices and
sufferings involved in doing
God's will in this life, who
see beyond the passing
things of this world.

In the beatitudes Jesus turns the accepted values of the
world upside down. Rather than linking happiness with
accumulation and personal acclaim, Jesus says the "blessed"
or "happy" are those who love sacrificially and who suffer
for what is right. In the chart that follows, the first seven
beatitudes (in a different translation) are contrasted with
the values most men live by.

The Beatitudes   The Values Most Men Live By

How happy are the
humble-minded,
for the kingdom of
Heaven is theirs!

Happy are they
who have every-
thing they want,
for the world is
theirs.

Blessed are the
pushers: for they
get on in the
world.

How happy are
those who know
what sorrow
means, for they
shall be given
courage and
comfort!

Happy are the
hard guys who
never let life hurt
them, for they
never expect any-
thing and are
never disap-
pointed.

Blessed are the
hardboiled: for
they never let life
hurt them.

Happy are those
who claim noth-
ing, for the whole
earth will belong
to them!

Happy are they
who throw their
weight around, for
they get their way
in everything.

Blessed are they
who complain: for
they get their own
way in the end.

Happy are those
who are hungry
and thirsty for
goodness, for they
will be fully
satisfied!

Happy are they
who play it cool
with principles, for
they know which
side their bread
is buttered on.

Blessed are the
blasé: for they
never worry over
their sins.

Happy are the
merciful, for they
will have mercy
shown to them!

Happy are those
who don't tolerate
mistakes in any-
body, for they
get results.

Blessed are the
slave-drivers: for
they get results.

Happy are the
utterly sincere, for
they will see God!

Happy are the
dirty-minded, for
they see an angle
or a double mean-
ing in everything.

Blessed are the
knowledgeable
men of the world:
for they knew
their way around.

Happy are those who make peace, for they will be known as sons of God!	Happy are the troublemakers, for they get to be known as exciting.	Blessed are the troublemakers: for they make people take notice of them.
MATTHEW 5:3-9, PHILLIPS	From William J. Kalt and Ronald J. Wilkins, *To Live Is Christ,* Henry Regnery, 1965.	From J. B. Phillips, *Is God at Home?* Abingdon Press © 1957.

The leadership of Jewish society in Jesus' time had largely fallen into the hands of four groups. The *Pharisees* made religion a matter of following certain formal external laws; they took great pride in their meticulous observance of outward regulations and thought of themselves as superior to all others. The *Scribes* are usually associated with the Pharisees. They were the lawyers who busied themselves, as professionals, with the formalities of the law. The *Sadducees* were the priestly aristocracy and the wealthy who believed that their birth and background made them the chosen of God; they were worldly skeptics and had comparatively little interest in the minute details of the law. The *Zealots* had nationalized the Jewish religion. They sought a revolution overthrowing the Roman occupation and restoring Jewish rule.

Jesus' teachings are at variance with all four parties. Goodness to the Scribes and Pharisees was essentially negative: They maintained that a person was good if he avoided certain crimes (theft, murder, dietary uncleanness, etc.). They were concerned with outward acts. In contrast, Jesus' concept of goodness is *positive:* a man is good if his life radiates agape. In Jesus' view the goodness of an act is determined by the *motive behind it,* which must be agape. He takes one Old Testament law after another and contrasts it (by saying, "But what I tell you is this") with the new law. Jesus' law is harder because it is concerned not just with actions but with the motives behind acts. The new law, in a nutshell, is that everything we do must have agape as its motive.

Jesus asks us to look behind every act for its cause. For example, he seeks to get behind the act of murder to the root of what divides men.

"For I tell you, if your virtue goes no deeper than that of the scribes and Pharisees, you will never get into the kingdom of heaven. You have learned how it was said to our ancestors: *You must not kill;* and if anyone does kill he must answer for it before the court. But what I tell you is this: Anyone who nurses anger against his brother must be brought to judgement."

MATTHEW 5:20-21, JERUSALEM; 5:22, NEB

Jesus goes to the heart of the matter. Murder is the most extreme outgrowth of an inner anger and hatred. Jesus focuses on that inner attitude and tells his followers it is anger which they must struggle to control and overcome. From a man consumed with anger, only destructive words and actions can come. The man who nurses anger, who will not forget or forgive, excludes agape as the motivating factor in his life and makes reconciliation with his brother impossible. Jesus discards the old law's concept of vengeful justice and urges us to regard ourselves and our rights as secondary in importance. Our first obligation is to let agape determine how we act.

'You have learned that they were told, "an eye for an eye, and a tooth for a tooth." But what I tell you is this: Do not set yourself against the man who wrongs you. If someone slaps you on the right cheek, turn and offer him your left. If a man wants to sue you for your shirt, let him have your coat as well. If a man in authority makes you go one mile, go with him two. Give when you are asked to give; and do not turn your back on a man who wants to borrow.'

MATTHEW 5:38-42

This is not a weak, cowardly yielding to wickedness, but a positive principle of action, with the motive and purpose of reconciling an enemy. Sometimes, of course, it is necessary for individuals and nations to use force to demonstrate agape. Corporal punishment by a parent is sometimes the most effective way of expressing love and concern; some wars are "just" in that they are fought to protect innocent people and to resist evil. But more often than we think, perhaps, turning the other cheek is the best way of reconciling those who seek to hurt us.

Agape is the essence of all that Jesus teaches.

'You have learned that they were told, "Love your neighbor, hate your enemy." But what I tell you is this: Love your enemies and pray for your persecutors; only so can you be children of your heavenly Father, who makes the sun rise on good and bad alike, and sends the rain on the honest and the dishonest. If you love only those who love you, what reward can you expect? Surely the taxgatherers do as much as that. And if you greet only your brothers, what is there extraordinary about that? Even the heathen do as much. You must therefore be all goodness, just as your heavenly Father is all good.'

MATTHEW 5:43-48

To love our enemies is not necessarily to agree with them or to approve what they are doing. Reconciliation should never be confused with blurring the distinction between right and wrong. But Jesus points out that if our hearts are hate-filled we will not seek to persuade or reconcile an enemy, but only to alienate him further. Jesus said "abhor that which is evil." But he also said "Love him who treats you cruelly." Even though a person may hurt us, we can still seek to turn his heart and to reach out for him as a human being.

The Sermon
on the Mount–2

6

Jesus contrasts the old law and the new. Whereas the old law emphasized appearance, the new law is concerned with the motive behind all outward acts. Jesus takes the three principal religious practices of Judaism—almsgiving, prayer, and fasting—as illustrations. He points out first how almsgiving can have the wrong motivation by a desire to win praise from men, the motive being not agape but self-gain.

'Be careful not to make a show of your religion before men; if you do, no reward awaits you in your Father's house in heaven. Thus, when you do some act of charity, do not announce it with a flourish of trumpets, as the hypocrites do in synagogue and in the streets to win admiration from men. I tell you this: they have their reward already. No; when you do some act of charity, do not let your left hand know what your right hand is doing; your good deed must be secret, and your Father who sees what is done in secret will reward you.'

MATTHEW 6:1-4

The giver of alms can be certain that his gift is genuinely motivated by agape if he gives it secretly, so that others cannot know about it or praise him for it. Prayer, too, can be wrongly motivated. It can become a mere formality, the recital of words. People can use it in order to appear pious and to gain the praise of men. Jesus calls those whose prayer is a mere show "hypocrites," the Greek word for actors.

41

'Again, when you pray, do not be like the hypocrites; they
love to say their prayers standing up in the synagogue and at
street-corners for everyone to see them. I tell you this: they
have their reward already. But when you pray, go into a room
by yourself, shut the door, and pray to your Father who is there
in the secret place.'   MATTHEW 6:5-6

In response to the disciples' request that he teach them to
pray, Jesus illustrates, with his own prayer, what prayer
should be. It is not pious words, but the lifting up of our lives
to God. It is not something done to impress men, but an
offering to God. It is not an attempt to manipulate God, but
to give our lives to God that he may use us as instruments
of his love. The Lord's Prayer is so central to Jesus' thought
and being that we will consider each phrase of it separately.

Our Father. From the time of his baptism on, the fatherhood
of God is the center of Christ's thought. He never addressed God by any other title than Father. Jesus regarded
religion not as a formality but as a relationship, a relationship such as that between father and son. The incomprehensible power which created and sustains the universe
is not just sheer force; it is also personal. God is not an
abstraction or a principle; he is like a father. He gives us
life, he cares about us, hears us, chastises us, provides for
us. And, since he is the Father of us all (not "my Father"
but "our Father"), we are all brothers.

Who art in Heaven. This phrase reminds us that we are
temporary creatures on earth, limited by time and space,
certain of death. God is infinitely beyond our understanding
—eternal. Heaven is not a geographical place, but a state
of being which transcends the material, and in which time
and place have no existence. We sometimes think of ourselves as all-powerful and immortal. We can become so
immersed in applauding ourselves that we forget to lift up
our lives to what is truly lasting and valuable.

Hallowed be Thy Name. We are but little specks on a speck
in the universe, here today and gone tomorrow. We therefore come before God (who orders all things) with respect,
recognizing our limitations, and cherishing our relationship to him.

Thy Kingdom come. Kingdom means *control* or *rule.* Every
man's life is ruled by something: acquisition, pleasure,
fame, popularity. Jesus teaches us that our lives would be
happiest if we let God's law of love rule them, not later
but now.

Thy will be done, on earth as it is Heaven. These words
explain what "Thy Kingdom come" means. We are the
means by which God's fatherhood and his reconciling love
are made known. St. Francis of Assisi paraphrased these
words in his own prayer: "Lord, make me an instrument
of Thy peace."

Give us this day our daily bread. We ask only for the basic
necessities, and only for today. Prayer is not a means of
manipulating God into giving us material benefits. Of the
material things in life, we ask only for the bare essentials.

*And forgive us the wrong we have done, as we have forgiven
those who have wronged us.* We can ask God to forgive
our failure to do his will only if we have been willing to
try to understand and love those whose conduct toward
us has been less than perfect.

*And let us not be led into temptation, but deliver us from
evil.* The wise man realistically recognizes that throughout
life he will be confronted by great temptations. We acknowledge that they will befall us, and we ask for strength
to overcome what tempts us.

After the Lord's Prayer Jesus discusses the religious custom
of fasting or self-denial. The Pharisees made a great parade
of their twice-weekly public fast. Jesus pointed out their
hypocrisy.

'So too when you fast, do not look gloomy like the hypocrites: they make their faces unsightly so that other people may
see that they are fasting. I tell you this: they have their reward
already. But when you fast, anoint your head and wash your
face, so that men may not see that you are fasting, but only
your Father who is in the secret place.'   MATTHEW 6:16-18

Again, only if a man denies himself in secret can he be sure
that his motive is self-sacrifice and not the gaining of men's
praise.

Jesus turns next to our attitude toward material things,
which should be one of detachment. Jesus nowhere condemns
material possessions, he only reminds us that we can become
so engrossed in them that we forget their temporary nature
and cease to seek what is truly lasting.

'Do not store up for yourselves treasure on earth, where it
grows rusty and moth-eaten, and thieves break in to steal it.
Store up treasure in heaven, where there is no moth and no
rust to spoil it, no thieves to break in and steal. For where your
treasure is, there will your heart be also. . . . No servant can
be the slave of two masters; for either he will hate the first and
love the second, or he will be devoted to the first and think
nothing of the second. You cannot serve God and Money.'
                                         MATTHEW 6:19-21, 24

The person who has in a clear-cut way made up his mind
to serve God first is freed from the anxious preoccupation
with money and possessions which characterizes so many
people.

'Therefore I bid you put away anxious thoughts about food
and drink to keep you alive, and clothes to cover your body.
Surely life is more than food, the body more than clothes. Look
at the birds of the air; they do not sow and reap and store in
barns, yet your heavenly Father feeds them. You are worth

more than the birds! Is there a man of you who by anxious thought can add a foot to his height? And why be anxious about clothes? Consider how the lilies grow in the fields; they do not work, they do not spin; and yet, I tell you, even Solomon in all his splendour was not attired like one of these. But if that is how God clothes the grass in the fields, which is there today, and tomorrow is thrown on the stove, will he not all the more clothe you? How little faith you have! No, do not ask anxiously, "What are we to eat? What are we to drink? What shall we wear?" All these are things for the heathen to run after, not for you, because your heavenly Father knows that you need them all. Set your mind on God's kingdom and his justice before everything else, and all the rest will come to you as well. So do not be anxious about tomorrow; tomorrow will look after itself. Each day has troubles enough of its own.'

MATTHEW 6:25-34

This is an elaboration by Jesus on one of the petitions of his prayer: "Give us today our daily bread." Jesus does not condemn prudent foresight; his concern is to point out the fruitlessness of sick worry. Augustine remarked that "to serve God is perfect freedom" in that we seek to live each day fully, as if it were the last, and never to become preoccupied with material concerns other than what are essential for life in the present.

One of the most destructive elements in human relationships is criticism. If we are determined to see the bad in others we will find it. Jesus urges us to "hate what is evil" whether it is in ourselves or in others. Yet Jesus tells us not to waste time judging other people. We cannot know what makes them act the way they do. We should look for and affirm the best in others, and see our own faults before we are critical of others.

'Pass no judgement, and you will not be judged. For as you judge others, so you will yourselves be judged, and whatever measure you deal out to others will be dealt back to you. Why do you look at the speck of sawdust in your brother's eye, with never a thought for the great plank in your own? Or how can you say to your brother, "Let me take the speck out of your eye," when all the time there is that plank in your own? You hypocrite! First take the plank out of your own eye, and then you will see clearly to take the speck out of your brother's.'

MATTHEW 7:1-5

The old law, and indeed all of Jewish tradition and history, is summarized and fulfilled in the Golden Rule of agape:

'Always treat others as you would like them to treat you: that is the Law and the prophets.'   MATTHEW 7:12

Jesus says that men will be his disciples to the extent that they practice agape in their lives: 'You will recognize them by the fruits they bear. Not everyone who calls me "Lord, Lord" will enter the kingdom of Heaven, but only those who do the will of my heavenly Father' (Matthew 7:16, 21). Jesus reminds his disciples of their calling:

'You are salt to the world. And if salt becomes tasteless, how is its saltness to be restored? It is now good for nothing but to be thrown away and trodden underfoot.'   MATTHEW 5:13

Salt, though it is tiny, insignificant in size, nevertheless changes the whole flavor of a meal. So the disciples, though few in number, are called to change the flavor of the society in which they live. In the ancient world salt was used to prevent rotting, as a preservative. Such is the effect which those who love can have on society.

Miracles 7

What are miracles? We may begin with a working definition. A miracle is an occurrence which man, at this present stage of development, cannot explain in terms of his present understanding of the laws of nature.

"Science" is what we call our present observation and understanding of the way things happen in nature. We find nature regular and predictable and we call this regularity "scientific law." We note that if an object is dropped it will, under normal circumstances, fall. Since we see this happen regularly we call it a "scientific law," in this case the law of gravity.

Scientists never say (or, more properly, never should say) that something cannot happen. Scientists say only that it has not happened in our observation and is therefore not likely to happen. If your great-great-grandfather has been told that a person could sit in New York and talk to someone in London, he would probably have said, "Impossible!" Such a thing, however, is not impossible; the telephone makes it possible. He would have been more accurate if he had said, "It *does* not happen at this time that people sitting in New York talk to people sitting in London, and I cannot imagine that such a thing ever will happen."

There are some interesting occasions upon which scientists have foolishly said something "*cannot* happen" rather than "*does* not (in our present observation) happen." One thinks of the physicists who dogmatically asserted that "the atom *cannot* be split." And then it was. Michael Bruce described an incident in London some years ago involving the Australian Duckbill Platypus "which has a bill like a duck, webbed feet and lays eggs, but also has fur and suckles its young. When the first stuffed specimen was exhibited at the Royal Society, all the biologists laughed and said it was a very good hoax and they could not see where it was sewn together; but they couldn't be taken in, and there was no such animal. Some of them said it was scientifically impossible. Then someone caught one of them alive." (Michael Bruce, *No Empty Creed*, Seabury, 1965, pp. 43-44)

Scientific "law" is constantly changing as we observe nature more deeply. What is said to violate scientific law at one point often becomes a cardinal scientific law at a future point. An occurrence which appears to be unexplainable by scientific law in one era is easily explainable by the scientific law of another era. Men have progressively changed the "laws" of science as they more fully observe and understand nature.

Human Potential

Scientists estimate that even the brightest human beings use less than twenty percent of their brain capacity today. The potential is there, but for some reason man has not yet tapped it and put it to use. Most of us operate at about twelve to thirteen percent of brain capacity. When we meet a mathematical genius, someone with a computer-like mind (someone perhaps using eighteen percent of his brain capacity), we say: "He's a real wizard!" or more likely "What a weirdo!" We mean he's not normal, he's not human. But, of course, he is human; he is more human than we are in that he is making much more use of his human potential than we are able to make. Imagine the things that would become natural and normal to man if he could use twenty-five or thirty percent of his brain capacity!

History records a number of lives remarkable for their richness and fullness, but none more uniquely rich and full than Christ's. Somehow his human capacities were freed for use, released. And, as a result, he did things which, to the rest of us, are not normal or natural. We do not, of course, fully understand why or how Jesus' capabilities, unlike our own, were unlocked. We do know from our own experience, though, that we can do things in some circumstances better than we can do them in others: "I'm too tired; I'll do it another time" or "You're making me nervous; I can't concentrate" or "The coach really lectured us at half time and we went out and tore up the field." Our human capacities are more easily released in one circumstance than in another. A few years ago at a university two boys carried a heavy safe down two flights of stairs to safety out of a burning building. The next day they couldn't even push the safe along the ground. The crisis had caused their glands to secrete adrenalin and they were able to pick up the safe. They could do something in one situation they couldn't do in another.

Jesus' life shows what happens when human life is put in a new situation, when man lets God act through him. Latent capacities are vitalized and hidden capabilities released. Jesus shows that when human life is open and attuned to God, what is natural and normal for man changes.

A Look at Three of Jesus' Miracles

One of the first people Jesus encountered as he traveled around was a leper. Perhaps no affliction is as disgusting and frightening to man as rotting bones and skin. Lepers had to carry bells and everywhere they went they had to shout "Unclean!" No respectable Jew would have dreamt of getting near a leper; in fact, it was against the law.

And a leper came to him beseeching him, and kneeling said to him, "If you will, you can make me clean." Moved with pity,

he stretched out his hand and touched him, and said to him "I
will; be clean." And immediately the leprosy left him, and he
was made clean.   MARK 1:40-42, RSV

Jesus does not force the miracle on him. The leper senses that
Christ is a person to whom he can turn for help. It is very
difficult to help a person unless he both desires to be helped
and believes that he can be helped. The leper expresses both
the desire ("beseeching him") and the confident faith ("if
you will, you can"). Obeying the higher law of love, Jesus
breaks the established law, extends his hand and touches the
leper. In compassion Jesus reaches out to the leper in his
desolate isolation. Then Jesus closes the encounter.

Then he dismissed him with this stern warning: 'Be sure you
say nothing to anybody. Go and show yourself to the priest,
and make the offering laid down by Moses for your cleansing;
that will certify the cure.'   MARK 1:43-44

Jesus repeats this strict warning ("say nothing to any one")
almost every time he heals someone. He repeats it because he
did miracles not to call attention to himself or to attract followers, but only out of compassionate love for an afflicted
person. Some people have asserted that Jesus did miracles to
prove he was divine. But there were so many sorcerers and
magicians in the ancient world performing apparently exotic
acts that no man of Jesus' own time would have attributed
divinity to him upon witnessing a miracle. And if we today
saw someone heal a leper we would hardly jump to the conclusion that he was divine. Jesus' miracles are love responding to need. Again and again he urges those who have been
healed to be silent.

In marked contrast to the pathetic Jewish leper outcast, a
ranking officer of the Roman occupation army sends Jesus a
request.

When he had finished addressing the people, he went to Capernaum. A centurian there had a servant whom he valued highly; this servant was ill and near to death. Hearing about Jesus, he sent some Jewish elders with the request that he would come and save his servant's life. They approached Jesus and pressed their peitition earnestly: 'He deserves this favour from you,' they said, 'for he is a friend of our nation and it is he who built us our synagogue.'   LUKE 7:1-5

Two things distinguish the centurion: the extent to which he is prepared to go because of his deep concern about his servant, and his unusual generosity in helping the Jews build their synagogue.

So Jesus went with them, and was not very far from the house when the centurion sent word to him by some friends: 'Sir,' he said, 'do not put yourself to trouble; because I am not worthy to have you under my roof; and that is why I did not presume to approach you in person. But say the word and my servant will be cured. I know, for in my position I am myself under orders, with soldiers under me. I say to one, "Go", and he goes; to another, "Come here", and he comes; and to my servant, "Do this," and he does it.'
LUKE 7:6, JERUSALEM; 7:7-8, NEB

Here is a powerful man—a chief of the occupation, a revered military leader—and yet one is struck by his humility: "I exercise certain powers," he says in effect, "and I sense in you a great and powerful authority—I know you can heal my servant. Though I have done nothing to deserve it, I ask your help."

When Jesus heard these words he was astonished at him and, turning around, said to the crowd following him, 'I tell you, not even in Israel have I found faith like this'. And when the messengers got back to the house they found the servant in perfect health.   LUKE 7:9-10, JERUSALEM

Though the servant is made well, the crowd with Jesus does not witness it or even know about it. The messengers only find out after they have returned. Because of the centurion's great desire and strong faith, Jesus heals the servant.

On another occasion they brought him a man who was deaf and, therefore, unable to speak intelligibly, and they asked him to heal him.

Jesus took him away from the crowd by himself. He put his fingers in the man's ears and touched his tongue with his own saliva.   MARK 7:33, PHILLIPS

Taking him away from the excited crowd to calm him, Jesus communicates with the man by the only language he could understand: touch and sign. He establishes contact, gets through to him.

Then, looking up to heaven, he sighed, and said to him, 'Ephphatha', which means [in Aramaic], 'Be opened.' And his ears were opened and immediately whatever had tied his tongue came loose and he spoke quite plainly. Jesus gave instructions that they should tell no one about this happening.
                                            MARK 7:34 NEB; 7:35-36, PHILLIPS

We see only the isolation resulting from the man's deafness; we do not know its medical cause. We only know that Jesus, with his developed human sensitivity and insight, finds a way literally to open up a life previously closed by deafness to relationships.

Jesus' Followers Called to Do Miracles

Jesus not only expected but commanded his disciples to do miracles:

Then he called his twelve disciples to him and gave them authority to cast out unclean spirits and to cure every kind of ailment and disease. MATTHEW 10:1

'He who has faith in me will do what I am doing; and he will do greater things still." JOHN 14:12

These twelve Jesus sent out with the following instructions: 'Go. And as you go proclaim the message: "The kingdom of Heaven is upon you." Heal the sick, raise the dead, cleanse the lepers, cast out devils.' MATTHEW 10:5-8 (abridged)

These statements bother us somehow, probably because we picture a huge faith healing with television cameras and millions watching, a side show. But that, of course, was not at all what Jesus had in mind. When we look back at those incidents where Jesus' human capabilities—his love and serenity and authority—were released to transform lives, the first thing we sense is the privateness and quietness with which they took place. What Jesus must have had in mind, then, is each one of us individually letting the power and love of God flow through us, awakening our human capabilities so that we can reach out to another individual. The last 2000 years have witnessed countless lives transformed by another person. And it happens today:

—A bank teller volunteers his time to join the Big Brother movement, and is assigned to a fourteen-year-old delinquent in a detention home. Encountering bitter hostility at first, and then apparent apathy, the teller persists in reaching out to the boy who seems deaf to every overture. Finally, after about a year, the boy comes to trust him and a relationship develops. The boy is healed, restored, able to finish high school and go to college.

—A successful businessman destroys his life by becoming an alcoholic. His family leaves him and he loses his job. Isolated and despairing he accepts the offered help of a friend, a former alcoholic. The former alcoholic spends hours each day and often in the middle of the night to help the man resist temptation and create a new life.

—An inner-city child grows up in a huge family where she receives almost no attention. When she becomes of school age she is classified as "retarded" and put in a class of nearly fifty in which she is an intolerable troublemaker. Then a volunteer, a housewife, meets her and reaches out to her. After months of hostility the girl begins to accept the volunteer's persistent love and after three years is able to be put in normal classes and take part in normal social activities.

One could offer countless examples of persons who, without the love of another individual, would have remained deaf or sick or dead. We cannot always explain fully how or why a person's compassion is sometimes able to transform another's life. We only know that it happens again and again.

When Jesus told us to heal the sick and cleanse the lepers, one of his intentions was to persuade us to look at life in terms of its possibilities. We are so often preoccupied with protecting ourselves from others and getting things for ourselves that we inhibit and cripple our human capabilities to reach out and love. Jesus urges us to dare to open ourselves, to dare to love, to see around the sick, the victims of society, the isolated, and to reach out and touch them. Never more than today, ironically, in our age of mass communication and instant access, have there been so many lepers, so many lonely, desolate individuals whose lives are waiting for us to reach out and touch them with understanding and compassion. Never more than today have there been so many who depend on us to seek help persistently for them. Never more than today have there been so many isolated by the deafness of mental illness or material hopelessness, the incapacity to live normal lives in society, who wait for us to stretch out our arms and reach them, and open up their lives again.

Jesus calls us as his disciples to open our eyes to the possibilities of life. To follow Christ is to do miracles, to touch and to change the lives of men by love, to let God's power into our lives to vitalize our human capabilities, to make the words, spoken first by Isaiah and then by Christ, our own.

The spirit of the Lord is upon me because he has anointed me; he has sent me to announce good news to the poor, to proclaim release for prisoners and recovery of sight for the blind; to let the broken victims go free, to proclaim the year of the Lord's favour.   LUKE 4:18-19

Water Into Wine 8

Jesus' life reveals the possibilities of human life. Nowhere is this clearer than in St. John's Gospel. John selects six of Christ's miracles to show the way Christ ennobles life and unfolds its possibilities. John sees each of these miracles on two levels. First, there is the simple event of the miracle itself, the power and love of God flowing through Jesus, enhancing his human capabilities and giving him power over nature and sickness. But John also sees each miracle as having a deeper meaning. He first tells of Jesus' presence at a wedding in Cana. At the celebration the wine runs out. We don't know why—whether through poverty or poor planning; but we do know that wine was the most important ingredient of a wedding reception and that to run out was a terrible humiliation.

On the third day there was a wedding at Cana-in-Galilee. The mother of Jesus was there, and Jesus and his disciples were guests also. The wine gave out, so Jesus's mother said to him, 'They have no wine left.' He answered, 'Your concern, mother, is not mine. My hour has not yet come.' His mother said to the servants, 'Do whatever he tells you.' There were six stone water-jars standing near, of the kind used for Jewish rites of purification; each held from twenty to thirty gallons. Jesus said to the servants, 'Fill the jars with water', and they filled them to the brim. 'Now draw some off', he ordered, 'and take it to the steward of the feast'; and they did so. The steward tasted the water now turned into wine, not knowing its source; though the servants who had drawn the water knew. He hailed the bridegroom and said, 'Everyone serves the best wine first, and waits until the guests have drunk freely before serving the poorer sort; but you have kept the best wine till now.'

JOHN 2:1-10

From one vantage point this is a "nature miracle." Man, as he has evolved, has exercised increasing control over nature and made more and more use of nature's potential. The potential for fire was always there; so was the atom's energy. But both remained unknown and unused until man developed his capabilities enough to unlock and use these natural forces. Jesus—his human capacities vitalized by his offering of his life to God—was able to do things in the natural world men had never done before.

But far more important is the insight we get into Jesus' personality. Some people picture Jesus as always serious and sombre, narrowly preoccupied with a great cause. Yet here we see him as the joyful participant in a country wedding, moved by his host's embarrassment. Note the quiet reserve with which the water is made wine, so that not even the steward knows the source. On a deeper level John means us to see this miracle as the symbol of all that Christ does: the ennobling of life, the turning of the water of existence into the wine of exuberant joyful life.

Again at Cana, John records that an official, prominent and powerful, presented himself to Jesus, the son of a village carpenter. One can imagine the humiliation this must have cost the officer.

An officer of the royal service was there, whose son was lying ill at Capernaum. When he heard that Jesus had come from Judaea into Galilee, he came to him and begged him to go down and cure his son, who was at the point of death. Jesus said to him, 'Will none of you ever believe without seeing signs and portents?'   JOHN 4:46-48

Jesus is by now leary of spectacle-seekers, and he responds to the official's request with seeming coldness, undoubtedly to test his sincerity. Jesus' question brings out the official's earnestness and his deep love for his son, expressed in an almost frenzied appeal.

The officer pleaded with him, 'Sir, come down before my boy dies.' Then Jesus said, 'Return home; your son will live.' The man believed what Jesus said and started for home. When he was on his way down his servants met him with the news, 'Your boy is going to live.' So he asked them what time it was when he began to recover. They said, 'Yesterday at one in the afternoon the fever left him.' The father noted that this was the exact time when Jesus had said to him, 'Your son will live', and he and all his household became believers.   JOHN 4:49-53

Again, the account's most outstanding characteristic is its restraint. There is not even conclusive evidence that a miracle occurred. Jesus may only have successfully predicted recovery on the basis of his understanding of the symptoms. But clearly, to the official, Jesus' intervention caused the change. Whatever literal significance the miracle may have, John sees a symbolic meaning as well. We cannot discover the possibilities of life unless we believe these possibilities exist. Faith—coming to Christ in humility and asking his help —is the beginning of a relationship in which our lives are ennobled and enriched.

Later, in Jerusalem to celebrate a religious holiday, Jesus encounters a pathetic figure who has been a paralytic for thirty-eight years and who, because of his paralysis, is not able to enter the baths which might have helped him.

Later on Jesus went up to Jerusalem for one of the Jewish festivals. Now at the Sheep-Pool in Jerusalem there is a place with five colonnades. Its name in the language of the Jews is Bethesda. In these colonnades there lay a crowd of sick people, blind, lame, and paralysed. Among them was a man who had been crippled for thirty-eight years. When Jesus saw him lying there and was aware that he had been ill a long time, he asked him, 'Do you want to recover?' 'Sir,' he replied, 'I have no one to put me in the pool when the water is disturbed, but while I am moving, someone else is in the pool before me.'

Jesus answered, 'Rise to your feet, take up your bed and walk.'
The man recovered instantly, took up his stretcher, and began
to walk.   JOHN 5:1-9

On the surface this miracle is like the other healings of Jesus.
But John means us to see the miracle as a parable: to see in
the paralytic our own human capabilities crippled by lack of
use or by misuse. To know Christ is to find our capacities
restored and revitalized. And certainly John wants us to take
Jesus' question to the paralytic, "Do you want to recover?"
as his question to us.

Along with all the other Gospel-writers, John records the
feeding of the 5000. A vast throng has come miles to hear
Jesus teach and they are hot and tired and hungry. Jesus'
sympathies are kindled at the sight.

Some time later Jesus withdrew to the farther shore of the
Sea of Galilee (or Tiberias), and a large crowd of people followed who had seen the signs he performed in healing the
sick. Then Jesus went up the hill-side and sat down with his
disciples. It was near the time of Passover, the great Jewish
festival. Raising his eyes and seeing a large crowd coming
towards him, Jesus said to Philip, 'Where are we to buy bread
to feed these people?' This he said to test him; Jesus himself
knew what he meant to do. Philip replied, 'Twenty pounds
would not buy enough bread for every one of them to have a
little.' One of his disciples, Andrew, the brother of Simon Peter,
said to him, 'There is a boy here who has five barley loaves and
two fishes; but what is that among so many?'   JOHN 6:1-9

Philip seems almost indignant at Jesus for suggesting so pre-
posterous an idea; Andrew is scarcely more positive, though
he does point out a boy who has five barley loaves and two
fishes. Jews usually carried sack-like baskets; this lad undoubtedly had packed in his these small provisions to eat
during the day. Barley loaves were roll-sized and were the

poor man's bread; the fish were undoubtedly the tiny sardine-like fish of the Sea of Galilee, usually preserved by being pickled. Though this boy had little, what he had he offered.

Jesus said, 'Make the people sit down.' There was plenty of grass there, so the men sat down, about five thousand of them. Then Jesus took the loaves, gave thanks, and distributed them to the people as they sat there. He did the same with the fishes, and they had as much as they wanted. When everyone had had enough, he said to his disciples, 'Collect the pieces left over, so that nothing may be lost.' This they did, and filled twelve baskets with the pieces left uneaten of the five barley loaves.

JOHN 6:10-13

There are many interpretations of what happened. For example, some say the people were fed not physically, but spiritually. However, this explanation requires leaving out much of the evidence. The most likely explanation is that Jesus pointed out the boy's willingness to share his modest lunch and this gave the people present (some of whom had undoubtedly brought food with them for the long journey out to the country) an impetus to share their food. That in itself—the changing of suspicious, selfish individuals into a sharing community—is no small achievement. Perhaps it was human nature which was altered, and not loaves and fishes. Others claim that Jesus literally multiplied the loaves and fishes, though actually there is no evidence of his doing this in the details of the story. We see no miracle itself; all we see is the difference that is plain after Jesus' intervention. At a deeper level John intends us to notice two things: First, the boy had the courage to offer his meagre lunch, even though it was (as Andrew pointed out) very little for so many. But Jesus takes that tiny offering and makes it the basis of everything. Clearly John wishes us to see how with Christ our little can become much. Secondly, John wants us to see Christ as the support and sustenance of our life; his life, his teachings, the possibilities he unfolds for us are the food by which we can live full, rich lives.

John turns next to Jesus' encounter with a man who had been born blind.

As he went on his way Jesus saw a man blind from his birth. His disciples put the question, 'Rabbi, who sinned, this man or his parents? Why was he born blind?' 'It is not that this man or his parents sinned,' Jesus answered; 'he was born blind so that God's power might be displayed in curing him.'

JOHN 9:1-3

Jesus rejects the primitive concept that sickness and deformity are the result of sin. Jesus' silence about why the man is blind is important. When we see the harsh realities of blindness, for example, or cancer, we often ask the fruitless unanswerable question: *Why?* And it sometimes becomes the occasion for cynicism and negativism about life. Jesus sees the man's blindness only as an occasion for compassion. We may not know the "whys" of life's problems, but Jesus shows us that we can respond with practical compassion to people as they cope with life's problems.

'While daylight lasts we must carry on the work of him who sent me; night comes, when no one can work. While I am in the world I am the light of the world.' With these words he spat on the ground and made a paste with the spittle; he spread it on the man's eyes, and said to him, 'Go and wash in the pool of Siloam.' (The name means 'sent'.) The man went away and washed, and when he returned he could see.   JOHN 9:4-7

On the surface this miracle is another illustration of Jesus' human capabilities being so highly developed that he was able to make a blind man see. At a deeper level the blind man perfectly symbolizes those who are helplessly living in a darkness from which they cannot escape through their own efforts. Jesus says, "I am the light of the world." His presence and touch bring men a vision of life's possibilities. By him the darkness of existence is turned into light.

The final miracle which John records is the raising of Lazarus from the dead. Lazarus of Bethany was the brother of Mary and Martha and all were friends of Jesus. The sisters sent word to Jesus that Lazarus was gravely ill. Jesus is delayed, but finally arrives.

On his arrival Jesus found that Lazarus had already been four days in the tomb. Bethany was just under two miles from Jerusalem, and many of the people had come from the city to Martha and Mary to condole with them on their brother's death. As soon as she heard that Jesus was on his way, Martha went to meet him, while Mary stayed at home. Martha said to Jesus, 'If you had been here, sir, my brother would not have died. Even now I know that whatever you ask of God, God will grant you.' Jesus said, 'Your brother will rise again.' 'I know that he will rise again', said Martha, 'at the resurrection on the last day.' Jesus said, 'I am the resurrection and I am life. If a man has faith in me, even though he die, he shall come to life; and no one who is alive and has faith shall ever die. Do you believe this?' 'Lord, I do,' she answered; 'I now believe that you are the Messiah, the Son of God who was to come into the world.'

With these words she went to call her sister Mary, and taking her aside, she said, 'The Master is here; he is asking for you.' When Mary heard this she rose up quickly and went to him. Jesus had not yet reached the village, but was still at the place where Martha left him. The Jews who were in the house condoling with Mary, when they saw her start up and leave the house, went after her, for they supposed that she was going to the tomb to weep there. So Mary came to the place where Jesus was. As soon as she caught sight of him she fell at his feet and said, 'O sir, if you had only been here my brother would not have died.' When Jesus saw her weeping and the

Jews her companions weeping, he sighed heavily and was deeply moved. 'Where have you laid him?' he asked. They replied, 'Come and see, sir.' Jesus wept.　　JOHN 11:17-35

Jesus never remained aloof from the sadness and tragedy of life; he was so immersed in it that, at times, as here, it drove him to tears of sorrow and despair.

The Jews said, 'How dearly he must have loved him!' But some of them said, 'Could not this man, who opened the blind man's eyes, have done something to keep Lazarus from dying?' Jesus again sighed deeply; then he went over to the tomb. It was a cave, with a stone placed against it. Jesus said, 'Take away the stone.' Martha, the dead man's sister, said to him, 'Sir, by now there will be a stench; he has been there four days.' Jesus said, 'Did I not tell you that if you have faith you will see the glory of God?' So they removed the stone. Then Jesus looked upwards and said, 'Father, I thank thee: thou hast heard me.' Then he raised his voice in a great cry: 'Lazarus, come forth.' The dead man came out, his hands and feet swathed in linen bands, his face wrapped in a cloth. Jesus said, 'Loose him; let him go.'　　JOHN 11:36-44 (abridged)

Some have suggested that Lazarus was in a catatonic trance, a mental state in which a person can appear to be dead, and that Jesus was able to restore him to a normal condition. But this goes against the massive evidence that Lazarus was really dead. Certainly John believed that Jesus' capabilities extended to control even over death. Whatever actually happened, John clearly sees this miracle as having a deeper meaning: it shows that Christ gives men life itself. There are many men leading meaningless existences, who are dead, entombed in life. To these Christ gives the opportunity to live: to come out of death, to be unbound and set free. In fact, to John, this climactic miracle summarizes all the miracles: in Christ men can rise from the deadness of their old existence to new life.

Jesus of Nazareth was not a military hero; he won no famous battles. He was not a political leader; he held no public office. He was not wealthy and powerful; he had no influence in the high places of the establishment. He did not teach in a university; he left behind no book. He left only a small band of followers.

Jesus attracted many listeners as he moved from place to place. Some of those who heard him were not content just to listen, but chose to follow him as disciples. A "disciple" is "one who is taught." Two young men, brothers, were among the first.

Jesus was walking by the Sea of Galilee when he saw two brothers, Simon called Peter and his brother Andrew, casting a net into the lake; for they were fishermen. Jesus said to them, 'Come with me, and I will make you fishers of men.' And at once they left their nets and followed him. He went on, and saw another pair of brothers, James son of Zebedee and his brother John; they were in the boat with their father Zebedee, overhauling their nets. He called them, and at once they left the boat and their father, and followed him.

MATTHEW 4:18-22

Most men attract followers by making promises. Jesus' promise is an unusual one: "Follow me and I will make you fishers of men." We can only guess at the personal magnetism that attracted these young brothers to leave their father and family business and follow Jesus. James and John were not rich or scholarly or famous; nor were they poor or outcasts. They were quite ordinary men, with ordinary talents. Jesus' appeal to them was that instead of using their talents to catch fish, they could use them in a greater cause.

As he became better known, Jesus attracted a larger and larger following of disciples. Out of this group he chose twelve as an inner circle and named them apostles (which means "those who are sent").

When day broke he called his disciples to him, and from among them he chose twelve and named them Apostles: Simon, to whom he gave the name of Peter, and Andrew his brother, James and John, Philip and Bartholomew, Matthew and Thomas, James son of Alphaeus, and Simon who was called the Zealot, Judas son of James, and Judas Iscariot who turned traitor.   LUKE 6:13-16

Of these twelve (whose number corresponds to the twelve tribes of Israel) not one was a man of influence or notable accomplishment.

From the outset, Jesus warns his followers not to be under any illusions about the way of life to which he has called them.

So Jesus went round all the towns and villages teaching in their synagogues, announcing the good news of the Kingdom, and curing every kind of ailment and disease. The sight of the people moved him to pity: they were like sheep without a shepherd, harassed and helpless; and he said to his disciples, 'The crop is heavy, but labourers are scarce; you must therefore beg the owner to send labourers to harvest his crop. Look, I send you out like sheep among wolves; be wary as serpents, innocent as doves. Provide no gold, silver, or copper to fill your purse, no pack for the road, no second coat, no shoes, no stick; the worker earns his keep.

'And be on your guard, for men will hand you over to their courts, they will flog you in the synagogues, and you will be brought before governors and kings, for my sake, to testify before them and the heathen. But when you are arrested, do not worry about what you are to say; when the time comes, the words you need will be given you; for it is not you who will be speaking: it will be the Spirit of your Father speaking in you. Brother will betray brother to death, and father his child; children will turn against their parents and send them to their death. All will hate you for your allegiance to me; but the man who holds out to the end will be saved. When you are persecuted in one town, take refuge in another. Do not fear those who kill the body, but cannot kill the soul. Fear him rather who is able to destroy both soul and body in hell.

'No man is worthy of me who cares more for father or mother than for me; no man is worthy of me who cares more for son or daughter; no man is worthy of me who does not take up his cross and walk in my footsteps. By gaining his life a man will lose it; by losing his life for my sake, he will gain it.'

MATTHEW 9:35—10:39 (abridged)

What Jesus promises his followers, then, is ridicule, suffering, danger, persecution, exhaustion, and poverty.

The costly sacrifice which discipleship involves is brought out most clearly, perhaps, in Jesus' encounter with a rich young man who, with oriental effusiveness, presents himself, asking what is the secret to full and happy living.

As he was starting out on a journey, a stranger ran up, and, kneeling before him, asked, 'Good Master, what must I do to win eternal life?' Jesus said to him, 'Why do you call me good? No one is good except God alone. You know the commandments: "Do not murder; do not commit adultery; do not steal; do not give false evidence; do not defraud; honour your father and mother." ' 'But, Master,' he replied, 'I have kept all these since I was a boy.' Jesus looked straight at him; his heart warmed to him, and he said, 'One thing you lack: go, sell everything you have, and give to the poor, and you will have riches in heaven; and come, follow me.' At these words his

face fell and he went away with a heavy heart; for he was a
man of great wealth.   MARK 10:17-22

Jesus instinctively recoils from the young man's flattery, and
his initial cold response warns the young man against glib-
ness and charm. In terms of the teaching of the Pharisees
and Sadducees, this young man was good: he broke none of
the commandments. Jesus, however, tells him that goodness
and happiness result not just from avoiding certain evils, but
rather from seeking opportunities to love. Jesus' words are
active and positive: go, sell, give, come, follow. The poor
that Jesus has in mind are not just the financially poor, but
those who are poor in health, in mind, in personality, in opportunity, in friends, in love. And wealth, obviously, is more
than money. Jesus calls us to give of our personalities and
abilities to those who need them. The young man comes
with an egocentric request: What can *I* do to be happy?
Jesus tells him that happiness results not from getting but
from giving.

Jesus never taught that wealth—financial or otherwise—
was intrinsically bad. He constantly emphasized that wealth
of any sort was a great responsibility. Wealth in terms of
money or ability places a heavy burden on the possessor to
use it correctly. In Jerusalem there was a very small gate. It
was known as the Needle because a camel had to lower himself to pass under it. Jesus uses the gate as an analogy.

Jesus looked round at his disciples and said to them, 'How
hard it will be for the wealthy to enter the kingdom of God!'
They were amazed that he should say this, but Jesus insisted,
'Children, how hard it is to enter the kingdom of God! It is
easier for a camel to pass through the eye of a needle than for
a rich man to enter the kingdom of God.'   MARK 10:23-25

We are born with certain abilities and into certain opportunities. We did nothing to earn these riches and opportuni-

ties. And we have them only for a time. Jesus tells the Parable of the Talents to illustrate that our riches are a sacred trust for which we are accountable.

'It is like a man going abroad, who called his servants and put his capital in their hands; to one he gave five bags of gold, to another two, to another one, each according to his capacity. Then he left the country. The man who had the five bags went at once and employed them in business, and made a profit of five bags, and the man who had the two bags made two. But the man who had been given one bag of gold went off and dug a hole in the ground, and hid his master's money. A long time afterwards their master returned, and proceeded to settle accounts with them. The man who had been given the five bags of gold came and produced the five he had made: "Master", he said, "you left five bags with me; look, I have made five more." "Well done, my good and trusty servant!" said the master. "You have proved trustworthy in a small way; I will now put you in charge of something big. Come and share your master's delight." The man with the two bags then came and said, "Master, you left two bags with me; look, I have made two more." "Well done, my good and trusty servant!" said the master. "You have proved trustworthy in a small way; I will now put you in charge of something big. Come and share your master's delight." Then the man who had been given one bag came and said, "Master, I knew you to be a hard man: you reap where you have not sown, you gather where you have not scattered; so I was afraid, and I went and hid your gold in the ground. Here it is—you have what belongs to you." "You lazy rascal!" said the master. "You knew that I reap where I have not sown, and gather where I have not scattered? Then you ought to have put my money on deposit, and on my return I should have got it back with interest. Take the bag of gold from him, and give it to the one with the ten bags. For the man who has will always be given more, till he has enough and to spare; and the man who has not will forfeit even what he has. Fling the useless servant out into the dark, the place of wailing and grinding of teeth!" '   MATTHEW 25:14-30

Our abilities are not museum pieces to be enjoyed; how we use the talents we have determines what kind of persons we are. Some have complained that Jesus criticized the least talented of the three men. This man had the best excuse: What can *I* do? I have so little power and influence. But Jesus deliberately singled him out. Most of us are one-talent people. We are not brilliant or powerful. We are the ones most tempted to irresponsible neglect of what abilities we have. A facet of the parable that is often overlooked is the reward which is given to the men who have used their talents: "I will put you in charge of something big." The reward is not ease and comfort; it is greater responsibility.

Discipleship–2

As Jesus' following grew, the Sadducees and Pharisees, leaders of the religious establishment (see chapter 5), became increasingly threatened by his popularity. First the Sadducees tried to humiliate him publicly by asking him questions. After the Sadducees failed to trap him, the Pharisees tried. The Pharisees believed religion was a matter of the strict observance of the 613 commandments of the Law. They held these 613 commandments, 365 of which were negative and 248 positive, to be each of equal importance. They therefore thought they would embarrass Jesus by asking him which commandment was the most important.

Hearing that he had silenced the Sadducees, the Pharisees met together; and one of their number tested him with this question: 'Master, which is the greatest commandment in the Law?' He answered, ' "Love the Lord your God with all your heart, with all your soul, with all your mind." That is the greatest commandment. It comes first. The second is like it: "Love your neighbour as yourself." Everything in the Law and the prophets hangs on these two commandments.'

MATTHEW 22:34-40

From the vast array of ritual, dietary, and moral laws in the Scriptures, Jesus with penetrating insight picks out two commandments, Deuteronomy 6:4–6 (Love God) and Leviticus 19:18 (Love neighbor), and says that they summarize all 613 commandments of the Law. He reiterates that true religion is concerned not with outward appearance, but with inward attitude. The essence of religion is not just avoiding certain evil acts, but positively and actively loving with our whole being.

Another Pharisee, a lawyer, puts a similar question to Jesus.

On one occasion a lawyer came forward to put this test question to him: 'Master, what must I do to inherit eternal life?' Jesus said, 'What is written in the Law? What is your reading of it?' He replied, 'Love the Lord your God with all your heart, with all your soul, with all your strength, and with all your mind; and your neighbour as yourself.' 'That is the right answer,' said Jesus: 'do that and you will live.' But he wanted to vindicate himself, so he said to Jesus, 'And who is my neighbour?'   LUKE 10:25-29

The Pharisee is no doubt more interested in carrying on a scholarly debate than in gaining insight. Jesus, however, refuses to enter into a learned discussion, and replies with a story.

Jesus replied, 'A man was on his way from Jerusalem down to Jericho when he fell in with robbers, who stripped thim, beat him, and went off leaving him half dead. It so happened that a priest was going down by the same road, but when he saw him, he went past on the other side. So too a Levite came to the place, and when he saw him went past on the other side. But a Samaritan who was making the journey came upon him, and when he saw him was moved to pity. He went up and bandaged his wounds, bathing them with oil and wine. Then he lifted him on to his own beast, brought him to an inn, and looked after him there. Next day he produced two silver pieces and gave them to the innkeeper, and said, "Look after him; and if you spend any more, I will repay you on my way back." Which of these three do you think was neighbour to the man who fell into the hands of the robbers?' He answered, 'The one who showed him kindness.' Jesus said, 'Go and do as he did.'   LUKE 10:30-37

For the hero of the story Jesus picks a Samaritan, a member of a detested minority group. The road to Jericho was notoriously dangerous; travelers were warned never to stop along the way. Thieves would often plant a decoy who pretended to be hurt and whose cries would lure a traveler off the road where he would be beaten and robbed. The Samaritan was probably a traveling merchant returning home to his family. If he stopped, he risked bodily harm and delay. We may imagine that the priest and Levite, to their way of thinking, had very "good excuses" for not stopping to help: perhaps they were on the way to some important task; perhaps they were able to convince themselves that stopping was not so much merciful as it was foolhardy. But the Samaritan took the risk, and Jesus singles him out as illustrating what it means to love one's neighbor as one's self. To love is often inconvenient, unpleasant, and even dangerous. And our neighbor is whoever needs our help, whether or not we know him.

In another parable, Jesus stresses the connection between the two great commandments, love of God and love of our neighbor.

'When the Son of Man comes in his glory and all the angels with him, he will sit in state on his throne, with all the nations gathered before him. He will separate men into two groups, as a shepherd separates the sheep from the goats, and he will place the sheep on his right hand and the goats on his left. Then the king will say to those on his right hand, "You have my Father's blessing; come, enter and possess the kingdom that has been ready for you since the world was made. For when I was hungry, you gave me food; when thirsty, you gave me drink; when I was a stranger you took me into your home, when naked you clothed me; when I was ill you came to my help, when in prison you visited me." Then the righteous will reply, "Lord, when was it that we saw you hungry and fed you, or thirsty and gave you drink, a stranger and took you home, or naked and clothed you? When did we see you ill or in prison, and come to visit you?" And the king will answer, "I tell you this: anything you did for one of my brothers here, however humble, you did for me." Then he will say to those on his left hand, "The curse is upon you; go from my sight to the eternal fire that is ready for the devil and his angels. For when I was hungry you gave me nothing to eat, when thirsty nothing to drink; when I was a stranger you gave me no home, when naked you did not clothe me; when I was ill and in prison you did not come to my help." And they too will reply, "Lord when was it that we saw you hungry or thirsty or a stranger or naked or ill or in prison, and did nothing for you?" And he will answer, "I tell you this: anything you did not do for one of these, however humble, you did not do for me." '

MATTHEW 25:31-45

The quality of our lives is determined by the love with which we respond to the individuals we encounter in the events of daily life. Perhaps reflecting on Jesus' words, St. John wrote: "If a man says, 'I love, God', while hating his brother, he is a liar. If he does not love the brother whom he has seen, it cannot be that he loves God whom he has not seen" (I John 4:20).

Discipleship Involves Forgiving

One of the marks of discipleship is a willingness to forgive. Forgiveness is not an easy-going attitude which blurs the distinction between right and wrong. Real forgiveness involves accepting and loving a person, without condoning any cruel or hateful actions in which he may engage. This distinction is most clearly brought out in Jesus' encounter with the adulterous woman.

He had taken his seat and was engaged in teaching them when the doctors of the law and the Pharisees brought in a woman caught committing adultery. Making her stand out in the

middle they said to him, 'Master, this woman was caught in
the very act of adultery. In the Law Moses has laid down that
such women are to be stoned. What do you say about it?' They
put the question as a test, hoping to frame a charge against
him. Jesus bent down and wrote with his finger on the ground.
                                                            JOHN 8:2-6

Jesus is doubtless disturbed by the arrogant superiority of
the ecclesiastics as they use this woman to prove a point.
Perhaps in order to conceal and relieve his anger, Jesus bends
down and doodles in the dirt.

    When they continued to press their question he sat up
straight and said, 'That one of you who is faultless shall throw
the first stone.' Then once again he bent down and wrote on the
ground. When they heard what he said, one by one they went
away, the eldest first; and Jesus was left alone, with the woman
still standing there. Jesus again sat up and said to the woman,
'Where are they? Has no one condemned you?' She answered,
'No one, sir.' Jesus said, 'Nor do I condemn you. You may go;
do not sin again.'   JOHN 8:7-11

The incident shows the natural delight men take in condemning others. Men rarely feel as self-righteous as when they
are making judgments on others. Jesus asks: "Which of you
is perfect?" He does not condone her act: "Go and sin no
more." But he refuses to condemn her and tries to recall her
to her essential human dignity. When we judge and condemn
a person, we see him in terms of his worst characteristics and
expect from him only evil; when we forgive a person we see
him in terms of his best characteristics and dare to hope for
good from him.

    Our natural inclination is to resent having to forgive
others, to be impatient and to condemn. Peter expresses this
to Jesus.

Then Peter came up and asked him, 'Lord, how often am I to forgive my brother if he goes on wronging me? As many as seven times?' Jesus replied, 'I do not say seven times; I say seventy times seven. The kingdom of Heaven, therefore, should be thought of in this way: There was once a king who decided to settle accounts with the men who served him. At the outset there appeared before him a man whose debt ran into millions. Since he had no means of paying, his master ordered him to be sold to meet the debt, with his wife, his children, and everything he had. The man fell prostrate at his master's feet. "Be patient with me," he said, "and I will pay in full"; and the master was so moved with pity that he let the man go and remitted the debt. But no sooner had the man gone out than he met a fellow-servant who owed him a few pounds; and catching hold of him he gripped him by the throat and said, "Pay me what you owe." The man fell at his fellow-servant's feet, and begged him, "Be patient with me, and I will pay you"; but he refused, and had him jailed until he should pay the debt. The other servants were deeply distressed when they saw what had happened, and they went to their master and told him the whole story. He accordingly sent for the man. "You scoundrel!" he said to him, "I remitted the whole of your debt when you appealed to me; were you not bound to show your fellow-servant the same pity as I showed you?" And so angry was the master that he condemned the man to torture until he should pay the debt in full. And that is how my heavenly Father will deal with you, unless you each forgive your brother from your hearts.'   MATTHEW 18:21-35

Peter probably expected Jesus to tell him how generous he was to forgive someone as many as seven times. Jesus' response must have seemed cutting: by implication Jesus reminds Peter that he is not perfect, and that he can expect to be forgiven only to the extent that he is ready to forgive. What greater message could there be to a world torn by suspicion and hostility than this positive attitude of understanding, forgiveness, and reconciliation? How easy it is, though, for us to say, "Well, if that's the way he's going to be about it, I won't have anything to do with him!"

The Pharisees and Scribes refused to have anything to do with those who in any way broke the law; they smugly sought opportunities to demonstrate their own superiority by condemning others. They naturally were threatened by Jesus' attempt to reach out to sinners.

Another time, the tax-gatherers and other bad characters were all crowding in to listen to him; and the Pharisees and the doctors of the law began grumbling among themselves: 'This fellow', they said, 'welcomes sinners and eats with them.' He answered them with this parable: 'If one of you has a hundred sheep and loses one of them, does he not leave the ninety-nine in the open pasture and go after the missing one until he has found it? How delighted he is then! He lifts it on to his shoulders, and home he goes to call his friends and neighbours together. "Rejoice with me!" he cries. "I have found my lost sheep." In the same way, I tell you, there will be greater joy in heaven over one sinner who repents than over ninety-nine righteous people who do not need to repent.'   LUKE 15:1-7

Again Jesus reminds us that true happiness comes only from loving. A man can know no greater joy than to seek the person who has gone astray and to help him find himself and be restored to fullness of life. To forgive someone is to love him in spite of his faults and to help him see himself in terms of his highest potentials.

To be a disciple is to be called to follow, to be given responsibility. The Jews believed themselves the chosen people of God. Originally this meant that they were called by God to certain moral and spiritual obligations. But gradually many of the Jews took the "chosen" concept to mean not responsibility, but privilege. They came to assume that because they were Jews they were automatically God's chosen; they came to assume that by fulfilling certain outward pious ceremonies they would obtain credit in heaven. Jesus responded to them with a parable.

It was aimed at those who were sure of their own goodness and looked down on everyone else. 'Two men went up to the temple to pray, one a Pharisee and the other a tax-gatherer. The Pharisee stood up and prayed thus: "I thank thee, O God, that I am not like the rest of men, greedy, dishonest, adulterous; or, for that matter, like this tax-gatherer. I fast twice a week; I pay tithes on all that I get." But the other kept his distance and would not even raise his eyes to heaven, but beat upon his breast saying, "O God, have mercy on me, sinner that I am." It was this man, I tell you, and not the other, who went home acquitted of his sins. For everyone who exalts himself will be humbled; and whoever humbles himself will be exalted.'   LUKE 18:9-14

The Pharisee is not really offering a prayer of thanksgiving; he is congratulating himself. The intention of his prayer is to parade his virtues. The tax collector, as part of the graft-ridden Roman bureaucracy, was regarded as a traitor and outcast by fellow-Jews. Yet ironically he reveals the true spirit of prayer: the humble realization of our faults and limitations which is the prelude to letting God act through our lives. To be a disciple is not to make a claim on God, not to assume a privilege, but to accept a responsibility.

Jesus reiterates this theme in another story—the Parable of the Prodigal Son.

Again he said: 'There was once a man who had two sons; and the younger said to his father, "Father, give me my share of the property." So he divided his estate between them. A few days later the younger son turned the whole of his share into cash and left home for a distant country, where he squandered it in reckless living. He had spent it all, when a severe famine fell upon that country and be began to feel the pinch. So he went and attached himself to one of the local landowners, who sent him on to his farm to mind the pigs. He would have been glad to fill his belly with the pods that the pigs were eating; and no one gave him anything. Then he came to his senses and said, "How many of my father's paid servants have more food than they can eat, and here am I, starving to death! I will set off and go to my father and say to him, 'Father, I have sinned, against God and against you; I am no longer fit to be called your son; treat me as one of your paid servants.' " So he set out for his father's house. But while he was still a long way off his father saw him, and his heart went out to him. He ran to meet him, flung his arms around him, and kissed him. The son said, "Father, I have sinned, against God and against you; I am no longer fit to be called your son." But the father said to his servants, "Quick! fetch a robe, my best one, and put it on him; put a ring on his finger and shoes on his feet. Bring the fatted calf and kill it, and let us have a feast to celebrate the day. For this son of mine was dead and has come back to life; he was lost and is found." And the festivities began.

'Now the elder son was out on the farm; and on his way back, as he approached the house, he heard music and dancing. He called one of the servants and asked what it meant. The servant told him, "You brother has come home, and your father has killed the fatted calf because he has him back safe and sound." But he was angry and refused to go in. His father came out and pleaded with him; but he retorted, "You know how I have slaved for you all these years; I never once disobeyed your orders; and you never gave me so much as a kid, for a feast with my friends. But now that this son of yours turns up, after running through your money with his women, you kill the fatted calf for him." "My boy," said the father, "you are always with me, and everything I have is yours. How could we help celebrating this happy day? Your brother here was dead and has come back to life, was lost and is found." '

LUKE 15:11-32

Someone has said that this story should be called the Parable of the Loving Father. Even before the returning son has a chance to say his little speech, the father runs to embrace him. The older brother's view, however, is that of the self-righteous Pharisees who have nothing but contempt for those who have done something wrong. Somehow they feel their virtue is best brought out in comparison to the inadequacies of others. The older brother refers to the returning brother not as "my brother," but as "this son of yours," and then catalogues all his brother's vices. The older brother has apparently rendered service to his father not out of joy and love, but out of a grim and grudging desire to gain a claim on his father. The returning son makes no claim ("I am no longer fit to be called your son"), placing his life in his father's hands. Jesus reminds us that God is not an automatic vending machine whose reward we can calculate. Our love must be offered freely, trusting that God will take care of us in his own way.

Accepting God's Invitation

When we try to make a claim on God, we are attempting, in effect, to put God in a box, to manipulate him into acting a certain way if we do certain things. Jesus deals with this presumption in a parable about itinerant laborers who stand in the market place (where laborers were hired) hoping someone will employ them for the day.

'The kingdom of Heaven is like this. There was once a land-owner who went out early one morning to hire labourers for his vineyard; and after agreeing to pay them the usual day's wage he sent them off to work. Going out three hours later he saw some more men standing idle in the market-place. "Go and join the others in the vineyard," he said, "and I will pay you a fair wage"; so off they went. At midday he went out again, and at three in the afternoon, and made the same ar-rangement as before. An hour before sunset he went out and found another group standing there; so he said to them, "Why are you standing about like this all day with nothing to do?" "Because no one has hired us", they replied; so he told them, "Go and join the others in the vineyard." When evening fell, the owner of the vineyard said to his steward, "Call the labourers and give them their pay, beginning with those who came last and ending with the first." Those who had started work an hour before sunset came forward, and were paid the full day's wage. When it was the turn of the men who had come first, they expected something extra, but were paid the same amount as the others. As they took it, they grumbled at their employer: "These late-comers have done only one hour's work, yet you have put them on a level with us, who have sweated the whole day long in the blazing sun!" The owner turned to one of them and said, "My friend, I am not being unfair to you. You agreed on the usual wage for the day, did you not? Take your pay and go home. I choose to pay the last man the same as you. Surely I am free to do what I like with my own money. Why be jealous because I am kind?" '

MATTHEW 20:1-15

Without the landowner everyone in the story would have been unemployed. Some laborers he employs at the start of the day; they agree to the usual fair day's wage. In the end they are paid it; no injustice is done them. Later in the day the landowner hires another group of laborers who have been waiting. Those that he hired last he chooses to pay what is in effect more than the usual day's wage. With them he chooses, for reasons known only to himself, to be unusually generous. But the all-day laborers complain, even though no injustice has been done them. Most of us think of ourselves as the early-comers. We picture ourselves as virtuous and deserving. One question we must ask ourselves, though, is whether we really have labored all day as disciples. Perhaps most of us, honestly, must put ourselves among the late-comers and rejoice that God has been extravagantly generous to us in terms of our labor. God calls men at different times to labor as disciples in the vineyard of the world. We need not fear that, in the end, his wages will be unjust.

Jesus tells another parable about God's invitation, the Parable of the Sower. Some have said that it should be called the Parable of the Different Kinds of Soil. God sows the seeds; some soils accept it while others refuse.

That same day Jesus went out and sat by the lake-side, where so many people gathered round him that he had to get into a boat. He sat there, and all the people stood on the shore. He spoke to them in parables, at some length. He said: 'A sower went out to sow. And as he sowed, some seed fell along the footpath; and the birds came and ate it up. Some seed fell on rocky ground, where it had little soil; it sprouted quickly because it had no depth of earth; but when the sun rose the young corn was scorched, and as it had no root it withered away. Some seed fell among thistles; and the thistles shot up, and choked the corn. And some of the seed fell into good soil, where it bore fruit, yielding a hundredfold or, it might be sixty-fold or thirtyfold. If you have ears, then hear. . . . You then, may hear the parable of the sower. When a man hears the word that tells of the Kingdom but fails to understand it, the evil one comes and carries off what has been sown in his heart. There you have the seed sown along the footpath. The seed sown on rocky ground stands for the man who, on hearing the word, accepts it at once with joy; but as it strikes no root in him he has no staying-power, and when there is trouble or persecution on account of the word he falls away at once. The seed sown among thistles represents the man who hears the word, but worldly cares and the false glamour of wealth choke it, and it proves barren. But the seed that fell into good soil is the man who hears the word and understands it, who accordingly bears fruit, and yields a hundredfold or, it may be, sixtyfold or thirty-fold.'   MATTHEW 13:1-9, 18-23

Jesus undoubtedly told this parable to his disciples when they came to him discouraged about the apparent failure of their labors. Jesus begins with the realistic acknowledgment that much of the seed they sow will not take root. That is not the fault of the sower or the seed. God forces himself on no one; some lives will refuse him. Yet Jesus encourages his disciples to persist, even though there are no signs of success. For sometimes the seed that a disciple sows will fall into soil that accepts it, in which case the harvest will be vastly beyond anything he might have hoped for.

The seed will always be sown in the midst of weeds.

Here is another parable that he put before them: 'The kingdom of Heaven is like this. A man sowed his field with good seed; but while everyone was asleep his enemy came, sowed darnel among the wheat, and made off. When the wheat sprouted and began to fill out, the darnel could be seen among it. The farmer's men went to their master and said, "Sir, was it not good seed that you sowed in your field? Then where has the darnel come from?" "This is an enemy's doing", he replied. "Well then," they said, "shall we go and gather the darnel?" "No," he answered; "in gathering it you might pull up the wheat at the same time. Let them both grow together till harvest; and at harvest-time I will tell the reapers, 'Gather the darnel first, and tie it in bundles for burning; then collect the wheat into my barn.' " '   MATTHEW 13:24-30

Darnel is a type of weed which until its ripening at harvest time closely resembles wheat. Jesus was realistic about evil. He knew how evil men could be. He knew how hard it is to distinguish those who are truly good from those who only appear to be. Jesus tells us that it is impossible for us to try to judge the one from the other. Yet at the same time he assures us that ultimately judgment will be made by God. In the meantime it is fruitless for us to waste time and energy being angry and judgmental. Our task is to get on with our own labors.

Finally Jesus addresses a word to his disciples about persistence and endurance. Though we may give our whole lives and all we possess to the service of God and man, our efforts may appear to achieve little result.

He said also, 'How shall we picture the kingdom of God, or by what parable shall we describe it? It is like the mustard-seed, which is smaller than any seed in the ground at its sowing. But once sown, it springs up and grows taller than any other plant, and forms branches so large that the birds can settle in its shade.'   MARK 4:30-32

Even when a small seed is sown in good soil it may take many months for it to appear above ground. But when it does, it flowers into a bush thousands of times its original size. Jesus reminds his disciples that the farmer does not stop planting seeds if they do not blossom at once; rather he goes on patiently sowing his seed though no sign of any blossom appears for weeks. So it shall be with the disciples' efforts. They may be small. No sign of success may be observed immediately. But in the end the harvest will be vast beyond all expectations.

Jesus
the Messiah

Jesus' sincerity and power attracted many followers. But the Scribes and Pharisees were jealous and hostile. They resented this upstart with no formal education. The purity of his life showed up their hypocrisy. The sunshine of Jesus' early ministry is now clouded over by controversy. Responding to the Pharisees' claim that they are Abraham's children and therefore God's favorites:

'If you were Abraham's children', Jesus replied, 'you would do as Abraham did.' They said, 'We are not base-born; God is our Father, and God alone.' Jesus said, 'If God were your father you would love me, for God is the source of my being, and from him I come. I speak the truth and therefore you do not believe me. Which of you convicts me of sin?'   JOHN 8:39, 41-42, 45

When they challenge the truth of what Jesus teaches, Jesus offers his life as evidence for the truth of what he says. And even his enemies could point to no defect in his character. It is, in fact, the very sincerity of his life that so threatens the Scribes and Pharisees. Jesus continues:

'He who has God for his father listens to the words of God. You are not God's children; that is why you do not listen.' The Jews answered, 'Are we not right in saying that you are a Samaritan, and that you are possessed?' 'I am not possessed,' said Jesus; 'I am honouring my Father, but you dishonour me. I do not care about my own glory; there is one who does care, and he is judge. In very truth I tell you, if anyone obeys my teaching he shall never know what it is to die.' The Jews said, 'Now we are certain that you are possessed. Abraham is dead; the prophets are dead; and yet you say, "If anyone obeys my teaching he shall not know what it is to die." Are you greater than our father Abraham, who is dead? The prophets are dead too. What do you claim to be?' Jesus replied, 'If I glorify myself, that glory of mine is worthless. It is the Father who glorifies me, he of whom you say, "He is our God", though you do not know him. But I know him; if I said that I did not know him I should be a liar like you. But in truth I know him and obey his word. Your father Abraham was overjoyed to see my day; he saw it and was glad.' The Jews protested, 'You are not yet fifty years old. How can you have seen Abraham?' Jesus said, 'In very truth I tell you, before Abraham was born, I am.'

JOHN 8:47-58

Nowhere in the Gospels does Jesus make as high a claim as he does here. He claims for himself and his teachings more authority than Abraham, the father of Judaism. And his life is offered as evidence. It is a claim which forces all who hear it, then and now, to decide whether Jesus was an imposter or the revealer of God himself. The response of the religious leaders is clear.

They picked up stones to throw at him, but Jesus was not to be seen; and he left the temple.   JOHN 8:59

After this incident, Jesus takes his disciples away from the crowd, and almost forces them to make up their minds about who he is.

When he came to the territory of Caesarea Philippi, Jesus asked his disciples, 'Who do men say that the Son of Man is?' They answered, 'Some say John the Baptist, others Elijah, others Jeremiah, or one of the prophets.' 'And you,' he asked, 'who do you say I am?' Simon Peter answered: 'You are the Messiah, the Son of the living God.'   MATTHEW 16:13-16

Messiah is a Hebrew word which means "the anointed one."
The Greek word for Messiah was *Christos* (Christ). For centuries the Jews had waited for the Messiah to deliver them
and reign over them as king. This then is the highest title
Peter could have given Jesus. Jesus replies that Peter's faith
is the foundation upon which he will build the society of his
followers, the Church.

> Then Jesus said: 'Simon son of Jonah, you are favoured in-
> deed! You did not learn that from mortal man; it was revealed
> to you by my heavenly Father. And I say this to you: You are
> Peter, the Rock; and on this rock I will build my church and
> the powers of death will never conquer it.'
>
> MATTHEW 16:17-18

Jesus' Idea of Messiahship

Immediately after Peter's confession of faith, Jesus "gave
his disciples strict orders not to tell anyone that he was the
Messiah" (Matthew 16:20). Though he had accepted the
title "Messiah" he did not wish to use the word publicly because most Jews pictured the longed-for Messiah as a great
warrior king. Jesus' concept of the Messiah is very different.

> From that time Jesus began to make it clear to his disciples
> that he had to go to Jerusalem, and there to suffer much from
> the elders, chief priests, and doctors of the law; to be put to
> death and to be raised again on the third day. At this Peter
> took him by the arm and began to rebuke him: 'Heaven for-
> bid!' he said. 'No, Lord, this shall never happen to you.' Then
> Jesus turned and said to Peter, 'Away with you, Satan; you are
> a stumbling-block to me. You think as men think, not as God
> thinks.'   MATTHEW 16:21-23

The idea of the Messiah's suffering and dying was abhorrent
to Peter and the other disciples. What Peter says tempts
Jesus, momentarily. Jesus envisions evading the coming con-

flict with the religious leadership. But he overcomes the temptation and rejects Peter's words as evil.

Jesus goes on to speak of the Messiah not as a battle hero or political leader, but as a servant who suffers and dies for the people. The Messiah is not a king, but rather a shepherd.

'I have come that men may have life, and may have it in all its fullness. I am the good shepherd; the good shepherd lays down his life for the sheep. The hireling, when he sees the wolf coming, abandons the sheep and runs away, because he is no shepherd and the sheep are not his. Then the wolf harries the flock and scatters the sheep. The man runs away because he is a hireling and cares nothing for the sheep. I am the good shepherd; I know my own sheep and my sheep know me— as the Father knows me and I know the Father—and I lay down my life for the sheep.'   JOHN 10:10-15

A famous stained-glass window in a New York church pictures Christ the Good Shepherd, staff in hand, serenely watching over a few happily grazing sheep. This placid country scene and the quiet and tender look on Jesus' face emphasize the devoted care of the loving shepherd for his sheep. However, when Jesus spoke of himself as the shepherd he had quite another thought in mind. He knew that being a shepherd meant endless hours of lonely watching, and that a shepherd was frequently in danger, protecting his sheep against wolves and other dangers. He knew that a good shepherd might even be killed protecting his sheep.

Jesus never promised that being his disciple would be easy. Those who follow him will share his destiny of suffering and sacrifice.

And to all he said, 'If anyone wishes to be a follower of mine, he must leave self behind; day after day he must take up his cross, and come with me. Whoever cares for his own safety is lost; but if a man will let himself be lost for my sake, that man is safe. What will a man gain by winning the whole world, at the cost of his true self? For whoever is ashamed of me and mine, the Son of Man will be ashamed of him, when he comes in his glory and the glory of the Father and the holy angels. And I tell you this: there are some of those standing here who will not taste death before they have seen the kingdom of God.'   LUKE 9:23-27

The Transfiguration

These words are symbolically fulfilled eight days later when Jesus takes three of his disciples with him to the mountainside to pray. Fully aware that the power structure intends to crush him, Jesus in the face of death renews the commitment made at his baptism.

About eight days after this conversation he took Peter, John, and James with him and went up into the hills to pray. And while he was praying the appearance of his face changed and his clothes became dazzling white. Suddenly there were two men talking with him; these were Moses and Elijah, who appeared in glory and spoke of his departure, the destiny he was to fulfil in Jerusalem. Meanwhile Peter and his companions had been in a deep sleep; but when they awoke, they saw his glory and the two men who stood beside him. And as these were moving away from Jesus, Peter said to him, 'Master, how good it is that we are here! Shall we make three shelters, one for you, one for Moses, and one for Elijah?'; but he spoke without knowing what he was saying. The words were still on his lips, when there came a cloud which cast a shadow over them; they were afraid as they entered the cloud, and from it came a voice: 'This is my Son, my Chosen; listen to him.' When the voice had spoken, Jesus was seen to be alone.   LUKE 9:28-36

This occurrence is called the Transfiguration because the disciples saw Jesus in a new light, transfigured. Occasionally we see someone in a way we never saw him before. A television newscaster recently interviewed a woman whose neighbor, a teenage boy, had rescued her son from a burning house, incurring terrible burns. She remarked, "I never thought he amounted to much before." Suddenly she saw him in a new light. At the Transfiguration the disciples saw Jesus in a new light. The Gospels describe the significance of the event with Old Testament symbolism: the cloud (the symbol of the divine presence), the change in the face, the high mountain, are all similar to Moses' encounter with God on Mount Sinai. The presence of Moses (through whom God gave the Law) and Elijah (the greatest of the prophets), both of whom the Old Testament speaks of as forerunners of the Messiah, indicates that Jesus is the fulfillment of all Judaism's expectations. The baptism, we noted in chapter 4, was the great moment of realization for Jesus and marked the start of his ministry. The same voice is heard at the Transfiguration and marks the disciples' moment of realization that Jesus is the Messiah.

For Jesus, as he prays for guidance, the Transfiguration confirms the calling he received at his baptism, and he now prepares to face the suffering and death that lie ahead. Calling the twelve together he tells them what will happen to him in Jerusalem.

He took the Twelve aside and said, 'We are now going up to Jerusalem; and all that was written by the prophets will come true for the Son of Man. He will be handed over to the foreign power. He will be mocked, maltreated, and spat upon. They will flog him and kill him. And on the third day he will rise again.' But they understood nothing of all this; they did not grasp what he was talking about; its meaning was concealed from them.   LUKE 18:31-34

The Gathering Storm

13

Jesus' idea of the role of the Messiah was different from that of most Jews. They looked forward to the Messiah as a king who would reign in earthly splendor, drive out the enemies of Judaism, and establish the Jewish religion everywhere on earth. Jesus viewed the Messiah as a humble servant who suffered and died for the people.

The Triumphal Entry

Although he realizes that the Jewish leaders are out to get him, Jesus proceeds to the heart of the nation: Jerusalem. Great crowds had already come to the city for the annual Passover festival. They longed to find a political and military hero who would lead a revolt and drive out the Romans who occupied Palestine. They hoped Jesus would be that leader, and they greeted him eagerly and warmly.

They were now nearing Jerusalem; and when they reached Bethphage at the Mount of Olives, Jesus sent two disciples with these instructions: 'Go to the village opposite, where you will at once find a donkey tethered with her foal beside her; untie them, and bring them to me. If anyone speaks to you, say, "Our Master needs them"; and he will let you take them at once.' This was in fulfilment of the prophecy which says, 'Tell the daughter of Zion, "Here is your king, who comes to you in gentleness, riding on an ass, riding on the foal of a beast of burden." ' The disciples went and did as Jesus had directed, and brought the donkey and her foal; they laid their cloaks on them and Jesus mounted. Crowds of people carpeted the road with their cloaks, and some cut branches from the trees to spread in his path. Then the crowd that went ahead and the others that came behind raised the shout: 'Hosanna to the Son of David! Hosanna in the heavens!' When he entered Jerusalem the whole city went wild with excitement. 'Who is this?' people asked, and the crowd replied, 'This is the prophet Jesus, from Nazareth in Galilee.'   MATTHEW 21:1-11

Jesus accepts the role of Messiah by riding in triumph into the capital, but he explicitly associates the role of Messiah with sacrifice and suffering. He rides not on horseback as a conquering hero, but on a donkey in humility as a servant. Instead of leading the hoped-for revolution, he proceeds directly to the temple, the militarily most unstrategic place in Jerusalem, right under the eye of the Roman garrison.

The Plot of the Religious Leaders

In the temple, instead of inflaming the people against the Romans, Jesus launches a cutting attack on the Jewish leaders.

So they came to Jerusalem, and he went into the temple and began driving out those who bought and sold in the temple. He upset the tables of the money-changers and the seats of the dealers in pigeons; and he would not allow anyone to use the temple court as a thoroughfare for carrying goods. Then he began to teach them, and said, 'Does not Scripture say, "My house shall be called a house of prayer for all the nations"? But you have made it a robbers' cave.' The chief priests and the doctors of the law heard of this and sought some means of making away with him; for they were afraid of him, because the whole crowd was spellbound by his teaching.

MARK 11:15-18

Children used to sing a song which began "Gentle Jesus, meek and mild." Though Jesus lays his hands on no one, he forcefully and vividly demonstrates his indignation at the materialist hypocrisy that the religious leaders have put in place of Judaism. He threatens the leaders' pocketbooks and terrifies them by his influence over the crowd. He also attacks the leadership's exclusivist attitude, asserting that God's love is for peoples of all nations.

The clash is the culmination of a long struggle. From the start Jesus' life and teachings were a threat to the established leadership. Before he arrived in Jerusalem, Jesus had Sabbath dinner at the house of a Pharisee.

When he noticed how the guests were trying to secure the places of honour, he spoke to them in a parable: 'When you are asked by someone to a wedding-feast, do not sit down in the place of honour. It may be that some person more distinguished than yourself has been invited; and the host will come and say to you, "Give this man your seat." Then you will look foolish as you begin to take the lowest place. No, when you receive an invitation, go and sit down in the lowest place, so that when your host comes he will say, "Come up higher, my friend." Then all your fellow-guests will see the respect in which you are held. For everyone who exalts himself will be humbled; and whoever humbles himself will be exalted.'

LUKE 14:7-11

The point of the parable was not missed by the Pharisees. Jesus was attacking their spiritual pride, their assumption that they were superior to others.

At the same dinner party Jesus told another parable. It alludes to the history of his own people, the Jews, who failed again and again to accept God's call to be his people. In this parable, Jesus tells the Pharisees that they have been chosen by God, invited to his feast, yet they have refused the invitation.

'A man was giving a big dinner party and had sent out many invitations. At dinner-time he sent his servant with a message for his guests, "Please come, everything is now ready." They began one and all to excuse themselves. The first said, "I have bought a piece of land, and I must go and look over it; please accept my apologies." The second said, "I have bought five yoke of oxen, and I am on my way to try them out; please accept my apologies." The next said, "I have just got married and for that reason I cannot come." When the servant came back he reported this to his master. The master of the house was angry and said to him, "Go out quickly into the streets and alleys of the town, and bring me in the poor, the crippled, the blind, and the lame." The servant said, "Sir, your orders have been carried out and there is still room." The master replied, "Go out on to the highways and along the hedgerows and make them come in; I want my house to be full. I tell you that not one of those who were invited shall taste my banquet." '

LUKE 14:16-24

Those who were originally invited (the upper class religious Jews, the chosen people) all have excuses which seem quite reasonable—property, business and domestic affairs. Men rarely have trouble inventing rational excuses for whatever they choose to do. The host, in the parable, then sends his servants to the people of the nearby town. These towns-people symbolize the Jewish nation. If the Jewish leaders refuse God's invitation, perhaps the humbler Jews will accept it. They do, but room still remains. The host then sends his servants into the countryside. Those outside the town sym-bolize the non-Jews. In the parable God does not send the Pharisees away; he wants them to come, but they refuse. The opportunity is given; they choose not to take advantage of it and thereby condemn themselves. The Pharisees could hardly have missed Jesus' point: the humble Jews and the non-Jews whom they scorn are better able to accept the invi-tation to God's banquet than are the self-satisfied Pharisees.

On another occasion, Jesus told a parable which effectively attacked the Pharisees' lack of concern about poverty and injustice.

'There was once a rich man, who dressed in purple and the finest linen, and feasted in great magnificence every day. At his gate, covered with sores, lay a poor man named Lazarus, who would have been glad to satisfy his hunger with the scraps from the rich man's table. Even the dogs used to come and lick his sores. One day the poor man died and was carried away by the angels to be with Abraham. The rich man also died and was buried, and in Hades, where he was in torment, he looked up; and there, far away, was Abraham with Lazarus close beside him. "Abraham, my father," he called out, "take pity on me! Send Lazarus to dip the tip of his finger in water, to cool my tongue, for I am in agony in this fire." But Abraham said, "Remember, my child, that all the good things fell to you while you were alive, and all the bad to Lazarus; now he has his consolation here and it is you who are in agony. But that is not all: there is a great chasm fixed between us; no one from our side who wants to reach you can cross it, and none may pass from your side to us." "Then, father," he replied, "will you send him to my father's house, where I have five brothers, to warn them, so that they too may not come to this place of torment?" But Abraham said, "They have Moses and the prophets; let them listen to them." "No, father Abraham," he replied, "but if someone from the dead visits them, they will repent." Abraham answered, "If they do not listen to Moses and the prophets they will pay no heed even if someone should rise from the dead." '   LUKE 16:19-31

The rich man is not blamed for being rich; he is not blamed for doing anything evil. His sin—the Pharisees' sin— is the sin of doing nothing, of neglect and omission. This parable is not intended as a blueprint of the afterlife. But in it Jesus makes one point with unmistakable clarity: there is an ultimate justice. Those who are rich—in personality, in intelligence, in money—have a heavy responsibility for the use of their riches. They determine their own ultimate well-being by how they exercise that responsibility.

In public, in the temple in Jerusalem, Jesus singles out the priests and elders for indictment, comparing them unfavorably to the despised Jews who collected money for the Romans.

'I tell you this: tax-gatherers and prostitutes are entering the kingdom of God ahead of you. For when John came to show you the right way to live, you did not believe him, but the tax-gatherers and postitutes did; and even when you had seen that, you did not change your minds and believe him. Listen to another parable. There was a landowner who planted a vineyard: he put a wall round it, hewed out a winepress, and built a watch-tower; then he let it out to vine-growers and went abroad.'   MATTHEW 21:31-33

The landowner, who symbolizes God, bestows upon the tenants (the religious leaders) a variety of blessings and responsibilities: a vineyard (the people of Israel), a winepress, and a guard tower. Then the landowner leaves (God really gives man freedom). After a lapse of time, the landowner sends his servants (who symbolize the prophets who constantly recalled Israel to moral responsibility) to collect the rent.

'When the vintage season approached, he sent his servants to the tenants to collect the produce due to him. But they took his servants and thrashed one, murdered another, and stoned a third. Again, he sent other servants, this time a larger number; and they did the same to them. At last he sent them his son. "They will respect my son", he said. But when they saw the son the tenants said to one another, "This is the heir; come on, let us kill him, and get his inheritance." And they took him, flung him out of the vineyard, and killed him. When the owner of the vineyard comes, how do you think he will deal with those tenants?' 'He will bring those bad men to a bad end', they answered, 'and hand the vineyard over to other tenants, who will let him have his share of the crop when the season comes.' Then Jesus said to them, 'Have you never read in the scriptures: "The stone which the builders rejected has become the main corner-stone. This is the Lord's doing, and it is wonderful in our eyes"? Therefore, I tell you, the kingdom of God will be taken away from you, and given to a nation that yields proper fruit.'   MATTHEW 21:34-43

The landowner is patient; he repeatedly attempts to persuade the tenants to act responsibly—God gives men freedom to refuse him. The parable reveals that Jesus now senses that his final fate as God's son will be to be refused and put to death. The religious leadership is under no illusions about the parable's meaning.

When the chief priests and Pharisees heard his parables, they saw that he was referring to them; they wanted to arrest him, but they were afraid of the people who looked on Jesus as a prophet.   MATTHEW 21:45-46

Judas' Betrayal

Jesus continued to teach in the temple each day. The Zealots who had hoped he would lead a revolution became increasingly angry at his refusal to do so. The temple salesmen who made money selling religious junk to the people found their business upset by him. And the religious leaders were threatened by his blunt attacks on their hypocrisy. The Pharisees and Sadducees, together with all the others who regarded Jesus as a menace, now decided to kill him. Yet they were afraid to seize him in public lest they provoke a popular demonstration on his behalf. One of Jesus' disciples, Judas, provides them with what they need.

Judas went to the chief priests and officers of the temple police to discuss ways and means of putting Jesus into their power. They were greatly pleased and undertook to pay him a sum of money. He agreed, and began to look out for an opportunity to betray him to them without collecting a crowd.

LUKE 22:4-6

Judas contracts to tell the chief priests where they can find Jesus at night, away from the crowds. We do not know what motivated Judas' betrayal. There are indications Judas was a lover of money and possibly a thief (see John 12:6). He was perhaps tired of the demands of discipleship, having no bed, no money, little food. It is most likely that he was a member of the Zealot party who hoped that Jesus would lead a revolution, and that he was now embittered because Jesus had not acted. Some have suggested that he hoped by this means to force Jesus into starting the revolution. Whatever the reason, Judas now seeks an opportunity to find Jesus alone so that he can be quietly arrested by the religious leaders.

The Last Supper and the Arrest

14

Though he had gone outside Jerusalem each night after teaching, Jesus makes different arrangements for Thursday evening. He arranges to celebrate the Passover with his disciples in the city that night, exactly twenty-four hours before the Passover holiday was officially to begin.

. . . his disciples said to him, 'Where would you like us to go and prepare for your Passover supper?' So he sent out two of his disciples with these instructions: 'Go into the city, and a man will meet you carrying a jar of water. Follow him, and when he enters a house give this message to the householder: "The Master says, 'Where is the room reserved for me to eat the Passover with my disciples?' " He will show you a large room upstairs, set out in readiness. Make the preparations for us there.' Then the disciples went off, and when they came into the city they found everything just as he had told them. So they prepared for Passover. MARK 14:12-16

So on Thursday evening the disciples gather with Jesus in the upper room to celebrate the Passover supper. When they were gathered, Jesus

took bread and, after giving thanks to God, broke it and said: 'This is my body which is for you; do this as a memorial of me.' In the same way, he took the cup after supper, and said: 'This cup is the new covenant sealed by my blood. Whenever you drink it, do this as a memorial of me.'
1 CORINTHIANS 11:23-25

'But mark this—my betrayer is here, his hand with mine on the table. For the Son of Man is going his appointed way; but alas for that man by whom he is betrayed!' At this they began to ask among themselves which of them it could possibly be who was to do this thing. LUKE 22:21-23

Jesus followed two common Jewish customs at the Last Supper:

1. He celebrated the Passover holiday with his disciples. This holiday, still a day away, was the Jewish equivalent of our Thanksgiving Day. It was a family day of grateful celebration of the safe passing-over of the Jews to safety and freedom from their enslavement in Egypt hundreds of years before.

2. The Last Supper was a *chaburah* or "fellowship meal," a Jewish family dinner which, like a modern dinner party, was preceded by drink and appetizers. Jesus, as head of this "family" of friends, gave thanks for all, blessed the meal and broke a common loaf of bread, distributing a bit to each person. At the end of the meal, again in accordance with the custom, Jesus gave thanks and passed around a cup of wine, the "cup of blessing," from which all drank.

But in the atmosphere of crisis and danger, and with emotions heightened as they always are at the last meal before a departure, Jesus transformed the usual Jewish customs and charged them with new meaning:

1. The Jewish custom was to slay and prepare lambs for the Friday night Passover meal. Jesus celebrated the feast a night early, on Thursday evening, when the lambs were not yet ready. In place of the lambs, he put bread and wine which he called "my Body and Blood." Jesus identifies his death with the death of the lambs sacrificed to God at the Passover and then eaten as sacred food. And of course Jesus was crucified on Friday afternoon at the very time the lambs were slain. Thus St. Paul says, "Christ our Passover is sacri-

ficed for us." And John the Baptist calls Jesus "the Lamb of God."

2. Jesus bids his friends to continue this fellowship meal: "Do this, as often as you eat and drink this bread and wine, in remembrance of me." The breaking of bread is the distinctive act in which he wishes us to recall his living presence.

Jesus' Farewell to His Disciples

Time remained, in the course of this farewell meal, for only a few final words. The law of love summarizes and ties together all that he has taught and done.

'My children, for a little longer I am with you; then you will look for me, and, as I told the Jews, I tell you now, where I am going you cannot come. I give you a new commandment: love one another; as I have loved you, so you are to love one another. If there is this love among you, then all will know that you are my disciples.'   JOHN 13:33-35

'I have spoken thus to you, so that my joy may be in you, and your joy complete. This is my commandment: love one another, as I have loved you. There is no greater love than this, that a man should lay down his life for his friends.'
JOHN 15:11-13

To the disciples, anxious and confused as they sense the horrors of the next few hours, he says:

'Set your troubled hearts at rest. Trust in God always; trust also in me. There are many dwelling-places in my Father's house; if it were not so I should have told you; for I am going there on purpose to prepare a place for you. And if I go and prepare a place for you, I shall come again and receive you to myself, so that where I am you may be also; and my way there is known to you.' Thomas said, 'Lord, we do not know where you are going, so how can we know the way?' Jesus replied, 'I am the way; I am the truth and I am life; no one comes to the Father except by me. If you knew me you would know my Father too. From now on you do know him; you have seen him.' Philip said to him, 'Lord, show us the Father and we ask no more.' Jesus answered, 'Have I been all this time with you, Philip, and you still do not know me? Anyone who has seen me has seen the Father.'   JOHN 14:1-9

When Thomas asks how they can believe what he is telling them, Jesus takes his own life as the authoritative evidence. The world has seen many teachers of ethics, but only one teacher has ever *lived* his own teachings in the way Jesus did. So completely was Jesus' life given to God that in looking at Jesus one sees God.

Jesus talks with his disciples about his relationship to them also. He speaks of it using the Old Testament image of the vine. Throughout the Old Testament Israel is referred to as God's chosen vineyard, though Israel fails again and again to bear fruit. Jesus calls himself the *True* Vine who shows what fruit men can bear if they give themselves to God completely. The disciples are called to be part of that vine.

'I am the real vine, and my Father is the gardener. Every barren branch of mine he cuts away; and every fruiting branch he cleans, to make it more fruitful still. You have already been cleansed by the word that I spoke to you. Dwell in me, as I in you. No branch can bear fruit by itself, but only if it remains united with the vine; no more can you bear fruit, unless you remain united with me.'   JOHN 15:1-4

And since they and he are one, they can expect to be subjected to hardship and suffering similar to his own.

'If the world hates you, it hated me first, as you know well. If you belonged to the world, the world would love its own; but because you do not belong to the world, because I have chosen you out of the world, for that reason the world hates you. Remember what I said: "A servant is not greater than his master." As they persecuted me, they will persecute you; they will follow your teaching as little as they have followed mine. It is on my account that they will treat you thus, because they do not know the One who sent me.'   JOHN 15:18-21

Selfless and loving people, by their mere existence, reveal the selfishnes of others, and therefore are never tolerated by the hypocritical.

Jesus is about to be crucified. Evil will appear to triumph over good. He warns the disciples that they will be scattered and disillusioned. Yet he assures them that if they have the courage to endure the pain and sorrow, their despair will change to joy.

'A little while, and you see me no more; again a little while, and you will see me.' Some of his disciples said to one another, 'What does he mean by this: "A little while, and you will not see me, and again a little while, and you will see me", and by this: "Because I am going to my Father"?' So they asked, 'What is this "little while" that he speaks of? We do not know what he means.'

Jesus knew that they were wanting to question him, and said 'Are you discussing what I said: "A little while, and you will not see me, and again a little while, and you will see me"? In very truth I tell you, you will weep and mourn, but the world will be glad. But though you will be plunged in grief, your grief will be turned to joy. A woman in labour is in pain because her time has come; but when the child is born she forgets the anguish in her joy that a man has been born into the world. So it is with you: for the moment you are sad at heart; but I shall see you again, and then you will be joyful, and no one shall rob you of your joy.'   JOHN 16:16-22

One of Jesus' most amazing characteristics was his intimate, yet realistic, understanding of his friends. He knew they would desert him, in spite of his warnings, and yet he still loved them.

'Look, the hour is coming, has indeed already come, when you are all to be scattered, each to his home, leaving me alone. Yet I am not alone, because the Father is with me. I have told you all this so that in me you may find peace. In the world you will have trouble. But courage! The victory is mine; I have conquered the world.'   JOHN 16:32-33

The Garden of Gethsemane

After supper, Jesus and his disciples go out to a nearby olive grove on the Mount of Olives. He knows how they will react under pressure.

And Jesus said, 'You will all fall from your faith; for it stands written: "I will strike the shepherd down and the sheep will be scattered." Nevertheless, after I am raised again I will go on before you into Galilee.' Peter answered, 'Everyone else may fall away, but I will not.' Jesus said, 'I tell you this: today, this very night, before the cock crows twice, you yourself will disown me three times.' But he insisted and repeated: 'Even if I must die with you, I will never disown you.' And they all said the same. When they reached a place called Gethsemane, he said to his disciples, 'Sit here while I pray.' And he took Peter and James and John with him. Horror and dismay came over him, and he said to them, 'My heart is ready to break with grief; stop here, and stay awake.' Then he went forward a little, threw himself on the ground, and prayed that, if it were possible, this hour might pass him by. 'Abba, Father,' he said, 'all things are possible to thee; take this cup away from me. Yet not what I will, but what thou wilt.'   MARK 14:27-36

"Abba" is a Hebrew name children use to express love and trust to their fathers. As a trusting child in the face of hideous

suffering, Jesus turns to this Father and asks him not to force
him to drink the cup of pain and death. (If ever a prayer
seemed unanswered, this was it.) And yet Jesus ends his
prayer with the ultimate self-surrender: "Thy will, not mine,
be done."

He came back and found them asleep; and he said to Peter,
'Asleep, Simon? Were you not able to keep awake for one
hour? Stay awake, all of you; and pray that you may be spared
the test. The spirit is willing, but the flesh is weak.' Once more
he went away and prayed. On his return he found them asleep
again, for their eyes were heavy; and they did not know how
to answer him. The third time he came and said to them, 'Still
sleeping? Still taking your ease? Enough! The hour has come.
The Son of Man is betrayed to sinful men. Up, let us go forward! My betrayer is upon us.' Suddenly, while he was still
speaking, Judas, one of the Twelve, appeared, and with him
was a crowd armed with swords and cudgels, sent by the
chief priests, lawyers, and elders. Now the traitor had agreed
with them upon a signal: 'The one I kiss is your man; seize
him and get him safely away.' When he reached the spot, he
stepped forward at once and said to Jesus, 'Rabbi', and kissed
him. Then they seized him and held him fast. One of the party
drew his sword, and struck at the High Priest's servant, cutting
off his ear. Then Jesus spoke: 'Do you take me for a bandit,
that you have come out with swords and cudgels to arrest me?
Day after day I was within your reach as I taught in the temple,
and you did not lay hands on me. But let the scriptures be fulfilled.' Then the disciples all deserted him and ran away.

MARK 14:37-50

Trial and Crucifixion 15

Because Jerusalem was under Roman rule, Jesus had a double trial. First, he was brought before the Jewish Council (called the Sanhedrin, composed of Scribes and Pharisees, dominated by the Sadducees). But the Council did not have power to execute him. This right belonged to the Roman governor who, in a second trial, would weigh the charges that were presented and make the final decision.

It was now quite late at night and the Jewish leaders took Jesus first to the house of Annas. Though his son-in-law, Caiaphas, was now high priest, Annas had been high priest and still remained the most powerful Jewish leader. He had grown rich by selling articles in the temple and no one wanted more to see Jesus out of the way.

The troops with their commander, and the Jewish police, now arrested Jesus and secured him. They took him first to Annas. Annas was father-in-law of Caiaphas, the High Priest for that year—the same Caiaphas who had advised the Jews that it would be to their interest if one man died for the whole people.

The High Priest questioned Jesus about his disciples and about what he taught. Jesus replied, 'I have spoken openly to all the world; I have always taught in synagogue and in the temple, where all Jews congregate; I have said nothing in secret. Why question me? Ask my hearers what I told them; they know what I said.' When he said this, one of the police struck him on the face, exclaiming, 'Is that the way to answer the High

Priest?' Jesus replied, 'If I spoke amiss, state it in evidence; if
I spoke well, why strike me?' So Annas sent him bound to
Caiaphas the High Priest.   JOHN 18:12-14, 19-24

At his house Caiaphas gathers a rump session of the Council in the middle of the night. Since he wishes to dispose of
Jesus as quietly and as quickly as possible, he gathers a few
Council members, holds unofficial court, and arranges for a
full early morning meeting of the Council to rubber-stamp
the verdict.

Then they led Jesus away to the High Priest's house, where
the chief priests, elders, and doctors of the law were all assem-
bling. Peter followed him at a distance right into the High
Priest's courtyard; and there remained, sitting among the at-
tendants, warming himself at the fire. The chief priests and the
whole Council tried to find some evidence against Jesus to
warrant a death-sentence, but failed to find any. Many gave
false evidence against him, but their statements did not tally.
Some stood up and gave false evidence against him to this
effect: 'We heard him say, "I will pull down this temple, made
with human hands, and in three days I will build another, not
made with hands." ' But even on this point their evidence did
not agree. Then the High Priest stood up in his place and questioned Jesus: 'Have you no answer to the charges that these
witnesses bring against you?' But he kept silence; he made
no reply.   MARK 14:53-61

Embarrassed by the fraudulence and contradictions of the
witnesses, Caiaphas tries to get Jesus to incriminate himself.

Again the High Priest questioned him: 'Are you the Messiah,
the Son of the Blessed One?' Jesus said, 'I am; and you will see
the Son of Man seated on the right hand of God and coming
with the clouds of heaven.' Then the High Priest tore his robes
and said, 'Need we call further witnesses? You have heard the
blasphemy. What is your opinion?' Their judgement was unan-

imous: that he was guilty and should be put to death. Some began to spit on him, blindfolded him, and struck him with their fists, crying out, 'Prophesy!' And the High Priest's men set upon him with blows.   MARK 14:61-65

By Jewish standards, everything about Jesus' trial was illegal. The Council did not meet in its chambers. The proceedings took place in the middle of the night and with great haste. No formal statement of charges was presented as required by law, and no witnesses for the defense were called. The prosecution and the jury were identical; the judge was the chief prosecutor.

Meanwhile Peter was still below in the courtyard. One of the High Priest's serving-maids came by and saw him there warming himself. She looked into his face and said, 'You were there too, with this man from Nazareth, this Jesus.' But he denied it: 'I know nothing,' he said; 'I do not understand what you mean.' Then he went outside into the porch; and the maid saw him there again and began to say to the bystanders, 'He is one of them'; and again he denied it. Again, a little later, the bystanders said to Peter, 'Surely you are one of them. You must be; you are a Galilean.' At this he broke out into curses, and with an oath he said, 'I do not know this man you speak of.' Then the cock crew a second time; and Peter remembered how Jesus had said to him, 'Before the cock crows twice you will disown me three times.' And he burst into tears.
                                                   MARK 14:66-72

Peter is the only disciple who did not run away; he enters into the lion's den of the high priest's courtyard. Even after one of the maids identifies him, he evades her question and remains. Yet, under pressure, he loses courage and denies any knowledge of Jesus.

At dawn the whole Council meets formally and decides to recommend the death penalty. Plans are quickly made to present Jesus to Pontius Pilate, the Roman procurator, who alone could inflict the death penalty.

As soon as morning came, the chief priests, having made their plan with the elders and lawyers in full Council, put Jesus in chains; then they led him away and handed him to Pilate.
                                                                    MARK 15:1

It was now early morning, and the Jews themselves stayed outside the headquarters to avoid defilement, so that they could eat the Passover meal. So Pilate went out to them and asked, 'What charge do you bring against this man?'   JOHN 18:28-29

They opened the case against him by saying, 'We found this man subverting our nation, opposing the payment of taxes to Caesar, and claiming to be Messiah, a king.'   LUKE 23:2

Before Pilate, the Jewish leaders base their case on grounds of treason. Pilate decides to examine Jesus privately.

Pilate then went back into his headquarters and summoned Jesus. 'Are you the king of the Jews?' he asked. Jesus said, 'Is that your own idea, or have others suggested it to you?' 'What! am I a Jew?' said Pilate. 'Your own nation and their chief priests have brought you before me. What have you done?' Jesus replied, 'My kingdom does not belong to this world. If it did, my followers would be fighting to save me from arrest by the Jews. My kingly authority comes from elsewhere.' 'You are a king, then?' said Pilate. Jesus answered, ' "King" is your word. My task is to bear witness to the truth. For this was I born; for this I came into the world, and all who are not deaf to truth listen to my voice.' Pilate said, 'What is truth?', and with those words went out again to the Jews.   JOHN 18:33-38

Pilate then said to the chief priests and the crowd, 'I find no case for this man to answer.' But they insisted: 'His teaching is causing disaffection among the people all through Judaea. It started from Galilee and has spread as far as this city.
                                                                    LUKE 23:4-5

Realizing Jesus is a Galilean, Pilate now sees a way out. He sends Jesus to King Herod, who ruled Galilee as a Roman protectorate.

When Pilate heard this, he asked if the man was a Galilean, and on learning that he belonged to Herod's jurisdiction he remitted the case to him, for Herod was also in Jerusalem at that time. When Herod saw Jesus he was greatly pleased; having heard about him, he had long been wanting to see him, and had been hoping to see some miracle performed by him. He questioned him at some length without getting any reply; but the chief priests and lawyers appeared and pressed the case against him vigorously. Then Herod and his troops treated him with contempt and ridicule, and sent him back to Pilate dressed in a gorgeous robe.   LUKE 23:6-11

Pilate again seeks to evade responsibility—this time by proposing a compromise.

Pilate now called together the chief priests, councillors, and people, and said to them, 'You brought this man before me on a charge of subversion. But, as you see, I have myself examined him in your presence and found nothing in him to support your charges. No more did Herod, for he has referred him back to us. Clearly he has done nothing to deserve death. I therefore propose to let him off with a flogging.'   LUKE 23:13-16

But the chief priests and councillors refuse to be put off. Pilate then tries another tactic.

At the festival season it was the Governor's custom to release one prisoner chosen by the people. There was then in custody a man of some notoriety, called Jesus Bar-Abbas. When they were assembled Pilate said to them, 'Which would you like me to release to you—Jesus Bar-Abbas, or Jesus called Messiah?' For he knew that it was out of spite that they had brought Jesus before him. While Pilate was sitting in court a message came to him from his wife: 'Have nothing to do with that innocent man; I was much troubled on his account in my dreams last night.' Meanwhile the chief priests and elders had persuaded the crowd to ask for the release of Bar-Abbas and to have Jesus put to death. So when the Governor asked, 'Which of the two do you wish me to release to you?', they said, 'Bar-Abbas.' 'Then what am I to do with Jesus called Messiah?' asked Pilate; and with one voice they answered, 'Crucify him!' 'Why, what harm has he done?' Pilate asked; but they shouted all the louder, 'Crucify him!'   MATTHEW 27:15-23

Going back into his headquarters he asked Jesus, 'Where have you come from?' But Jesus gave him no answer. 'Do you refuse to speak to me?' said Pilate. 'Surely you know that I have authority to release you, and I have authority to crucify you?' 'You would have no authority at all over me', Jesus replied, 'if it had not been granted you from above.'

JOHN 19:9-11

Jesus' calm silence and then the directness and simplicity of his response seem almost to put Pilate on trial. Confused and frightened by this obviously innocent man, Pilate makes one last effort to release him.

From that moment Pilate tried hard to release him; but the Jews kept shouting, 'If you let this man go, you are no friend to Caesar; any man who claims to be a king is defying Caesar.' When Pilate heard what they were saying, he brought Jesus out and took his seat on the tribunal at the place known as 'The Pavement' ('Gabbatha' in the language of the Jews). It was the eve of Passover, about noon. Pilate said to the Jews, 'Here is your king.' They shouted, 'Away with him! Away with him! Crucify him!' 'Crucify your king?' said Pilate. 'We have no king but Caesar', the Jews replied.   JOHN 19:12-15

Pilate could see that nothing was being gained, and a riot was starting; so he took water and washed his hands in full view of the people, saying, 'My hands are clean of this man's blood; see to that yourselves.' And with one voice the people cried, 'His blood be on us, and on our children.'

MATTHEW 27:24-25

The crowd settles it. Pilate dares not have reports of civil disturbances or rumors which question his Roman loyalty reach Rome. His job is threatened. The crowd in the court-yard, many of whom may have had a vested interest in selling articles in the temple, are whipped up to a frenzy of hatred by he chief priests and their henchmen. Finally Pilate crumbles.

Jesus had already been scourged (beaten by the soldiers with leather whips studded with sharp fragments of iron). Now he is mocked.

Pilate's soldiers then took Jesus into the Governor's head-quarters, where they collected the whole company round him. They stripped him and dressed him in a scarlet mantle; and plaiting a crown of thorns they placed it on his head, with a cane in his right hand. Falling on their knees before him they jeered at him: 'Hail, King of the Jews!' They spat on him, and used the cane to beat him about the head. When they had finished their mockery, they took off the mantle and dressed him in his own clothes.   MATTHEW 27:27-31

Jesus was now taken in charge and, carrying his own cross, went out to the Place of the Skull, as it is called (or, in the Jews' language, 'Golgotha'), where they crucified him, and with him two others, one on the right, one on the left, and Jesus between them.   JOHN 19:17-18

Crucifixion, the most degrading form of execution, was reserved by the Romans for slaves and the lowest of criminals. The victim was stripped and nailed hand and foot to the wood. Insects quickly gathered round the nail wounds and face and often ate away parts of the body while the helpless victim was still alive. Eventually shock and strangulation brought death.

And Pilate wrote an inscription to be fastened to the cross; it read, 'Jesus of Nazareth King of the Jews.' This inscription was read by many Jews, because the place where Jesus was crucified was not far from the city, and the inscription was in Hebrew, Latin, and Greek. Then the Jewish chief priests said to Pilate, 'You should not write "King of the Jews"; write, "He claimed to be king of the Jews." ' Pilate replied, 'What I have written, I have written.' The soldiers, having crucified Jesus, took possession of his clothes, and divided them into four parts, one for each soldier, leaving out the tunic. The tunic was seamless, woven in one piece throughout; so they said to one another, 'We must not tear this; let us toss for it'; and thus the text of Scripture came true: 'They shared my garments among them, and cast lots for my clothing.'   JOHN 19:19-24

There is no pain in human experience that Jesus did not suffer: the utmost physical torture, the mental despair of rejection and loneliness, and the triumphant scorn of his enemies.

The passers-by hurled abuse at him: 'Aha!' they cried, wagging their heads, 'you would pull the temple down, would you, and build it in three days? Come down from the cross and save yourself!' So too the chief priests and the doctors of the law jested with one another: 'He saved others,' they said, 'but he cannot save himself. Let the Messiah, the king of Israel, come down now from the cross. If we see that, we shall believe.' Even those who were crucified with him taunted him.

                                                    MARK 15:29-32

In agony upon the cross, Jesus cried out:

'Father, forgive them; they do not know what they are doing.'   LUKE 23:34

One of the criminals who hung there with him taunted him: 'Are not you the Messiah? Save yourself, and us.' But the other replied sharply, 'Have you no fear of God? You are under the same sentence as he. For us it is plain justice; we are paying the price for our misdeeds; but this man has done nothing wrong.' And he said, 'Jesus, remember me when you come to your throne.' He answered, 'I tell you this: today you shall be with me in Paradise.'   LUKE 23:39-43

But meanwhile near the cross where Jesus hung, stood his mother, with her sister, Mary, wife of Clopas, and Mary of Magdala. Jesus saw his mother, with the disciple whom he loved standing beside her. He said to her, 'Mother, there is your son'; and to the disciple, 'There is your mother'; and from that moment the disciple took her into his home.   JOHN 19:25-27

. . . and at three Jesus cried aloud, *'Eli, Eli, lema sabachthani?'* which means 'My God, my God, why hast thou forsaken me?'
MARK 15:34

After that, Jesus, aware that all had now come to its appointed end, said in fulfilment of Scripture, 'I thirst.' A jar stood there full of sour wine; so they soaked a sponge with the wine, fixed it on a javelin, and held it up to his lips. Having received the wine, he said, 'It is accomplished.'
JOHN 19:28-30

Then Jesus gave a loud cry and said, 'Father, into thy hands I commit my spirit'; and with these words he died.
LUKE 23:46

Jesus expresses his despair by uttering the first line of Psalm 22, in which God seems to reject the sufferer: "My God, my God, why hast thou forsaken me?" The words reflect his utter loneliness, his sense of failure, and even his loss of hope in God. And yet, in the end, he triumphs over that despair— "Father, into thy hands I commit my spirit."

The centurion saw it all, and gave praise to God. 'Beyond all doubt', he said, 'this man was innocent.' The crowd who had assembled for the spectacle, when they saw what had happened, went home beating their breasts.   LUKE 23:47-48

Because it was the eve of Passover, the Jews were anxious that the bodies should not remain on the cross for the coming Sabbath, since the Sabbath was a day of great solemnity; so they requested Pilate to have the legs broken and the bodies taken down. The soldiers accordingly came to the first of his fellow-victims and to the second, and broke their legs; but when they came to Jesus, they found that he was already dead, so they did not break his legs. But one of the soldiers stabbed his side with a lance, and at once there was a flow of blood and water.   JOHN 19:31-34

When evening fell, there came a man of Arimathaea, Joseph by name, who was a man of means, and had himself become a disciple of Jesus. He approached Pilate, and asked for the body of Jesus; and Pilate gave orders that he should have it. Joseph took the body, wrapped it in a clean linen sheet, and laid it in his own unused tomb, which he had cut out of the rock; he then rolled a large stone against the entrance, and went away. Mary of Magdala was there, and the other Mary, sitting opposite the grave. Next day, the morning after that Friday, the chief priests and the Pharisees came in a body to Pilate. 'Your Excellency,' they said, 'we recall how that impostor said while he was still alive, "I am to rise after three days." So will you give orders for the grave to be made secure until the third day? Otherwise his disciples may come, steal the body, and then tell the people that he has been raised from the dead; and the final deception will be worse than the first.' 'You may have your guard,' said Pilate; 'go and make it secure as best you can.' So they went and made the grave secure; they sealed the stone, and left the guard in charge.   MATTHEW 27:57-66

To the disciples the crucifixion was the ultimate proof of the triumph of evil over good. He on whom they had pinned their hopes and to whom they had committed their lives, was dead. He whom they had come to regard as sent from God had died the death of a common criminal. Bewildered, heart-broken and afraid, they either hid themselves or fled the city.

On the Sabbath (Saturday) it was improper to visit a tomb, but early on Sunday morning the women closest to Jesus went to his tomb to carry out the Jewish burial custom of anointing the body.

When the Sabbath was over, Mary of Magdala, Mary the mother of James, and Salome bought aromatic oils intending to go and anoint him; and very early on the Sunday morning, just after sunrise, they came to the tomb. They were wondering among themselves who would roll away the stone for them from the entrance to the tomb, when they looked up and saw that the stone, huge as it was, had been rolled back already. They went into the tomb, where they saw a youth sitting on the right-hand side, wearing a white robe; and they were dumbfounded. But he said to them, 'Fear nothing; you are looking for Jesus of Nazareth, who was crucified. He has been raised again; he is not here; look, there is the place where they laid him. But go and give this message to his disciples and Peter: "He is going on before you into Galilee; there you will see him, as he told you." ' Then they went out and ran away from the tomb, beside themselves with terror. They said nothing to anybody, for they were afraid.   MARK 16:1-8

Clearly Mary and the women were not expecting anything like a resurrection. They were confused because the body was missing and they found the young man's words incomprehensible. Bewildered and frightened they wait until they get back to Peter and John before they say anything about the body being gone.

"They have taken the Lord out of the tomb, and we do not know where they have laid him." Peter then came out with the other disciple, and they went toward the tomb. They both ran, but the other disciple outran Peter and reached the tomb first; and stooping to look in, he saw the linen cloths lying there, but he did not go in. Then Simon Peter came, following him, and he went into the tomb; he saw the linen cloths lying, and the napkin, which had been on his head, not lying with the linen cloths but rolled up in a place by itself. Then the other disciple, who reached the tomb first, also went in, and he saw and believed; for as yet they did not know the scripture, that he must rise from the dead.   JOHN 20:2-9, RSV

The other disciple "saw and believed." He did not believe that Jesus had risen; he believed the women's story that the tomb was empty. The empty tomb did *not* lead the disciples to assume that Jesus was risen from the dead. If we discovered an empty tomb, the last explanation we would consider is that the person buried in it had risen from the dead. Such was the case with the women and the disciples.

The Transformation of Jesus' Followers

After the disciples leave, Mary stands weeping at the tomb. Not only had Jesus been killed, but his body had been robbed from the tomb before it could be anointed. But then to Mary, in the depths of her grief and despair, an amazing thing happens.

So the disciples went home again; but Mary stood at the tomb outside, weeping. As she wept, she peered into the tomb; and she saw two angels in white sitting there, one at the head, and one at the feet, where the body of Jesus had lain. They said to her, 'Why are you weeping?' She answered, 'They have taken my Lord away, and I do not know where they have laid him.' With these words she turned round and saw Jesus standing there, but did not recognize him. Jesus said to her, 'Why are you weeping? Who is it you are looking for?' Thinking it was the gardener, she said, 'If it is you, sir, who removed him, tell me where you have laid him, and I will take him away.' Jesus said, 'Mary!' She turned to him and said, 'Rabbuni!' (which is Hebrew for 'My Master'). Jesus said, 'Do not cling to me, for I have not yet ascended to the Father. But go to my brothers, and tell them that I am now ascending to my Father and your Father, my God and your God.' Mary of Magdala went to the disciples with her news: 'I have seen the Lord!' she said, and gave them his message.   JOHN 20:10-18

Exuberant with excitement and joy, her whole outlook utterly transformed, Mary bursts in on the disciples and tells them that she has seen Jesus alive. We can imagine our reaction if someone told us he had seen a dead person alive. Luke (24:11) tells us how the disciples reacted: . . . "the story appeared to them to be nonsense, and they would not believe. . . ." The disciples remained secluded behind locked doors, still afraid they too would be arrested and put to death. Then suddenly they themselves also experience Jesus alive and present in their lives.

Late that Sunday evening, when the disciples were together behind locked doors, for fear of the Jews, Jesus came and stood among them. 'Peace be with you!' he said, and then showed them his hands and his side. So when the disciples saw the Lord, they were filled with joy.   JOHN 20:19-20

This experience of the living Christ transforms these despairing and frightened men into a joyful and courageous group and leaves them groping for words to describe their feelings. Two other disciples leaving Jerusalem earlier in the day also come to feel that Jesus is vividly and immediately with them. As they walk west into the sun they encounter a stranger.

That same day two of them were on their way to a village called Emmaus, which lay about seven miles from Jerusalem, and they were talking together about all these happenings. As they talked and discussed it with one another, Jesus himself came up and walked along with them; but something kept them from seeing who it was. He asked them, 'What is it you are debating as you walk?' They halted, their faces full of gloom, and one, called Cleopas, answered, 'Are you the only person staying in Jerusalem not to know what has happened there in the last few days?' 'What do you mean?' he said. 'All this about Jesus of Nazareth,' they replied, 'a prophet powerful in speech and action before God and the whole people; how our chief priests and rulers handed him over to be sentenced to death, and crucified him. But we had been hoping that he was the man to liberate Israel. What is more, this is the third day since it happened, and now some women of our company have astounded us: they went early to the tomb, but failed to find his body, and returned with a story that they had seen a vision of angels who told them he was alive. So some of our people went to the tomb and found things just as the women had said; but him they did not see.'

'How dull you are!' he answered. 'How slow to believe all that the prophets said! Was the Messiah not bound to suffer thus before entering upon his glory?' Then he began with Moses and all the prophets, and explained to them the passages which referred to himself in every part of the scriptures.

By this time they had reached the village to which they were going, and he made as if to continue his journey, but they pressed him: 'Stay with us, for evening draws on, and the day is almost over.' So he went in to stay with them. And when he had sat down with them at table, he took bread and said the blessing; he broke the bread, and offered it to them. Then their eyes were opened, and they recognized him; and he vanished from their sight. They said to one another, 'Did we not feel our

hearts on fire as he talked with us on the road and explained
the scriptures to us?'   LUKE 24:13-32

The two disciples, like Mary and the others, were obviously
not expecting a resurrection. Like Mary, they do not even
recognize Jesus at first. Jesus waits for their invitation and
then breaks bread with them, repeating the familiar gestures
of the last supper of a few days earlier. Doing what he told
them to do in remembrance of him, Jesus takes the bread,
blesses it, breaks it, and gives it to them, and they suddenly
recognize him. The two disciples spend all night returning to
Jerusalem where they find that the other disciples have also
experienced Jesus alive.

Without a moment's delay they set out and returned to
Jerusalem. There they found that the Eleven and the rest of the
company had assembled, and were saying, 'It is true: the Lord
has risen; he has appeared to Simon.' Then they gave their
account of the events of their journey and told how he had
been recognized by them at the breaking of bread.

As they were talking about all this, there he was, standing
among them. Startled and terrified, they thought they were seeing a ghost. But he said, 'Why are you so perturbed? Why do
questionings arise in your minds? Look at my hands and feet.
It is I myself. Touch me and see; no ghost has flesh and bones
as you can see that I have.' They were still unconvinced, still
wondering, for it seemed too good to be true. So he asked
them, 'Have you anything here to eat?' They offered him a
piece of fish they had cooked, which he took and ate before
their eyes.   LUKE 24:33-43

Luke, alone among the Gospel writers, emphasizes the real
bodily presence of Christ: he pictures Jesus standing among
the disciples. Jesus encourages them to touch his wounds and
he eats a piece of fish. Luke wants to show that the disciples
were not transformed by some imaginative vision, but by the
real presence of the living Christ.

Thomas is the last of the apostles to experience the risen Christ. Again, it is not the empty tomb, but Christ's vivid presence that convinces Thomas that Jesus is alive.

One of the Twelve, Thomas, that is 'the Twin', was not with the rest when Jesus came. So the disciples told him, 'We have seen the Lord.' He said, 'Unless I see the mark of the nails on his hands, unless I put my finger into the place where the nails were, and my hand into his side, I will not believe it.' A week later his disciples were again in the room, and Thomas was with them. Although the doors were locked, Jesus came and stood among them, saying, 'Peace be with you!' Then he said to Thomas, 'Reach your finger here: see my hands; reach your hand here and put it into my side. Be unbelieving no longer, but believe.' Thomas said, 'My Lord and my God!'

JOHN 20:24-28

Though Thomas is invited to touch Jesus' wounds he does not do so. Jesus' words emphasize that faith is not established by physical sight or evidence. Ironically, Thomas, whose doubts are the greatest, makes the most sweeping profession of belief in the end. Real faith is always strengthened by struggling with doubt.

Men experienced the risen Christ, but no one saw the Resurrection itself. The fact that Jesus was alive was made clear to different people in different ways at different times. The details of how he appeared vary from Gospel to Gospel. We know from our own experience that two different people can give amazingly different accounts of the same incident. Acts 1:3 tells us that to the apostles "he presented himself alive after his passion by *many* proofs" (RSV). Mary mistook him for the gardener and later was told by Jesus not to touch him. Thomas was told to touch his wounds. Close friends who walked with him to Emmaus did not recognize him till he broke bread. Other disciples recognized him instantly when he entered their quarters. We do not know exactly what kind of body Jesus appeared in after his resurrection: at times it appears to be ghostly, at other times physical.

We know only one thing for certain: some great event transformed a little group of despairing and frightened men into the most zealous and fearless body the world has ever known. The same men who hid in fear behind locked doors suddenly set out, full of superhuman confidence, to conquer the world. The details of this great event, which we call the Resurrection, are unimportant. The *fact* of the great event is immensely important. Something utterly changed the disciples. That something was their certainty that Jesus was alive, that though the world had put him to death, he had conquered death.

The crucifixion shows in an unmistakable way the tragedy and injustice of human earthly life. He whose life was utterly selfless and loving was crushed by selfishness and hate. Evil had triumphed over good. The Resurrection is the stunning reversal of that triumph. Unexpectant and reluctant as the disciples were, in their despair, to believe it, they became convinced that Jesus was not dead, but alive and present in their lives. Though the earthly powers of evil and death had been victorious, God had reversed their victory and Jesus was alive.

If the crucifixion had been the conclusion of Jesus' story, there would have been no more irrefutable proof in all history that the universe is unjust and absurd, that evil wins in the end. The Resurrection, however, proclaims that, though evil may triumph on earth, there is an ultimate justice and meaning in the universe, that good ultimately triumphs over evil. Transformed by and armed with this certainty, the disciples set out, fearless and bold, to tell the world about Jesus.

Though it is true that there is no such thing as impartial history, most modern historians try to approach historical events critically and impartially. Every historian has to select certain events to write about which he considers to be important. He determines what is important on the basis of certain principles. Different historians have different principles, so their accounts of the same historical incident may be different. They often accuse one another of prejudice. But most modern historians at least *attempt* a balanced and impartial study of historical events.

The New Testament writers do *not* try to be impartial. They do not pretend to present an objective account of Christianity. They are, in fact, highly partial and subjective. From the outset they proclaim their belief that Jesus' life reveals God in a unique way, and they write with the conviction that, though Jesus was put to death by men, God raised him from the dead and he is alive and present in their lives. The Resurrection is the central fact of their experience; the Resurrection is the reason that they write about Jesus.

Questioning the Evidence

We must keep in mind, therefore, as we consider the Resurrection, that the documents from which all the evidence comes are written by men absolutely convinced that Jesus was raised from the dead. Though there are no existing documents which present evidence against the Resurrection, a number of objections to it have been raised. They all involve questioning the honesty and integrity of the New Testament documents:

1. It is sometimes asserted that though the disciples underwent an inward change of attitude, no external event (rising from the dead) took place. In other words, the accounts of the Resurrection are mythological: the New Testament writers have invented external events to portray and demonstrate internal feelings. But this theory fails to explain *why* the disciples' inward attitude changed. They had no predisposition to change: they were utterly discouraged and afraid, they failed to comprehend Jesus' earlier references to the Resurrection, and when he rose from the dead they were slow to believe it even when it happened. Since there was no expectation of or predisposition to a change in attitude, some external event seems the most likely cause of their amazing transformation.

2. Some say the disciples did not really see Jesus alive, but only imagined they did. The New Testament accounts would then be imaginative fantasies. But how odd it is that they imagined something which they clearly did not expect! They were huddled behind locked doors in fear and despair, they rejected the women's experience in the garden as nonsense, and they were slow to recognize Jesus when he appeared to them. It is also extremely odd that so *many* would imagine they had seen Christ. As Paul remarked to King Agrippa (Acts 26:26): the Resurrection "was not done in a corner" (RSV). Paul even claims that Jesus not only appeared to the apostles, but that over 500 people saw him alive after his resurrection. Individual hallucinations are possible; but the idea of collective hallucinations is difficult to accept.

3. Others have asserted that the Resurrection is a story invented by Jesus' followers—a deliberate fraud. This theory assumes that all the disciples engaged in a deliberate act of deception and then all lied about it for the rest of their lives, not one of them ever revealing the secret. The enemies of Christianity made numerous attempts to torture the early Christians into denying the Resurrection; none ever succeeded in obtaining a confession of fraud. The New Testa-

ment shows the disciples were frequently stupid and weak. But even if we could assume that they were intelligent enough to devise this fraud and consistent enough to perpetrate it, we must still ask whether it is likely that Jesus' most intimate friends were deliberate and careful liars. Almost all of them were put to death for spreading the word about Jesus. How strange for them to have invented a lie for which they knew they would most likely be killed!

The suggestion that the apostles removed the body from the tomb to deceive others, even if it were true, proves nothing, since all the accounts show that the empty tomb convinced no one (including the disciples) that Jesus was alive; rather it was his supposed presence that convinced people.

4. It has been repeatedly suggested that Jesus never really died on the cross. This implies not only that the Jews and Romans, who wanted him dead, did not bother to make sure he was, but also that the apostles themselves were bold-faced liars. Leslie Weatherhead writes, "How could a person who had been scourged, tortured, nailed to a cross through the hot hours of the day, and into whose side a spear had been thrust, drawing not only blood but the water-like serum in the pericardial sac—itself proof of death—get off a stone slab, remove his own tightly wound wrappings and bandages, push back from the mouth of the cave-tomb a heavy grindstone-shaped boulder . . . which it took several strong men to move, evade the guards . . . , then appear to his friends not as an invalid needing weeks of nursing back to health, but as a triumphant conqueror over death who could . . . walk seven miles to Emmaus with his friends. . . ." Would such a figure not be tragic and pathetic rather than inspiring and victorious?

Summarizing the Evidence

The Resurrection cannot be proven or disproven by us. The most we can do is weigh the indications for and against it. We have looked at some of the objections advanced against the Resurrection; the Christian case for the Resurrection might be summarized as follows:

1. The Resurrection was the central fact of the preaching and writing of virtually all first-century Christians. They were prepared to face death to proclaim it to the world.

2. Something must account for the extraordinary transformation of the disciples. Something galvanized the frightened, fragmented, and shattered followers of Jesus into the zealous and courageous group that set out to conquer the world. Persecution and the threat of death served only to strengthen this body until finally it spread through the whole world.

3. But the most compelling indication of the Resurrection is the intuitive experience that people in the last 2000 years have had of the living Christ. Christ is not remembered by them as a dead hero; he is regarded as present in their lives.

Christians cannot prove Christ is alive. Such a thing is not subject to proof. A woman cannot prove her husband loves her. She may say, "He married me, he gives me all that I want, he seems happy to be with me," but these indications of love cannot prove his love. Christians do not claim to prove that Jesus is alive; they do seek to share their own experience. And they point to their experience and the experience of others as an indication that Christ rose from the dead.

Christ's Final Teachings

The Gospels appear to contradict one another on the length of Jesus' visible presence after the Resurrection. Most of the evidence indicates about forty days. "Forty days" in Greek (the language of the Gospels) is an idiom which indicates a vague period equivalent to "a couple of weeks" to us. The apostles, of course, had to go on earning a living in this period. Jesus was nonetheless present with them in the midst of their daily life and work.

Some time later, Jesus showed himself to his disciples once
again, by the Sea of Tiberias; and in this way. Simon Peter and
Thomas 'the Twin' were together with Nathanael of Cana-in-
Galilee. The sons of Zebedee and two other disciples were also
there. Simon Peter said, 'I am going out fishing.' 'We will go
with you', said the others. So they started and got into the
boat. But that night they caught nothing.

Morning came, and there stood Jesus on the beach, but the
disciples did not know that it was Jesus. He called out to them,
'Friends, have you caught anything?' They answered 'No.' He
said, 'Shoot the net to starboard, and you will make a catch.'
They did so, and found they could not haul the net aboard,
there were so many fish in it. Then the disciple whom Jesus
loved said to Peter, 'It is the Lord!' When Simon Peter heard
that, he wrapped his coat about him (for he had stripped) and
plunged into the sea. The rest of them came on in the boat,
towing the net full of fish; for they were not far from land,
only about a hundred yards.

When they came ashore, they saw a charcoal fire there, with
fish laid on it, and some bread. Jesus said, 'Bring some of your
catch.' Simon Peter went aboard and dragged the net to land,
full of big fish, a hundred and fifty-three of them; and yet,
many as they were, the net was not torn. Jesus said, 'Come and
have breakfast.' None of the disciples dared to ask 'Who are
you?' They knew it was the Lord. Jesus now came up, took the
bread, and gave it to them, and the fish in the same way.

JOHN 21:1-13

St. John sees in this account, as he often does, two levels
of meaning. A man standing on the shore of the Sea of
Tiberias can often see the location of schools of fish, whereas
those sailing on the lake cannot. This is still true today. Jesus,
appearing on the shore, is able to help the disciples make a
huge catch. They are surprised and embarrassed at first, but
Jesus puts them at ease by calmly making breakfast for them.
On a deeper level, John intends us to see that at the darkest
moments of life, when labor seems to bring no results ("that
night they caught nothing"), Christ is with us as guide and

helper. At Jesus' first encounter with the disciples, he said "Come with me, and I will make you fishers of men." Though the disciples have been through the dark night of the crucifixion, they are about to go forth into the world to make a huge "haul" of men.

Jesus then focuses on Peter, who, despite his denial of Christ, is the leader of the little band of apostles.

After breakfast, Jesus said to Simon Peter, 'Simon son of John, do you love me more than all else?' 'Yes, Lord,' he answered, 'you know that I love you.' 'Then feed my lambs', he said. A second time he asked, 'Simon son of John, do you love me?' 'Yes, Lord, you know I love you.' 'Then tend my sheep.' A third time he said, 'Simon son of John, do you love me?' Peter was hurt that he asked him a third time, 'Do you love me?' 'Lord,' he said, 'you know everything; you know I love you.' Jesus said, 'Feed my sheep.'   JOHN 21:15-17

Three times (the same number of times Peter had denied him) Jesus elicits the pledge of love from Peter. And each time Jesus responds by telling him that he can demonstrate this love by guiding and nourishing his sheep.

A strain of Jewish prophecy had seen the Messiah's coming as the time when Israel's rule over all the earth would be established and she would no longer be subjected by foreign powers.

So, when they were all together, they asked him, 'Lord, is this the time when you are to establish once again the sovereignty of Israel?' He answered, 'It is not for you to know about dates or times, which the Father has set within his own control. But you will receive power when the Holy Spirit comes upon you; and you will bear witness for me in Jerusalem, and all over Judaea and Samaria, and away to the ends of the earth.'
                                                      ACTS 1:6-8

Jesus' reply rebukes the disciples' crude political aspirations. God will reign at the end of time, but it will not be a political victory for any nation; and the time of God's reign is God's business not theirs. Their business—inspired by God's spirit, which is beyond nationality—will be to tell the world the good news about Jesus.

'Go therefore and make all nations my disciples; baptize men everywhere in the name of the Father and the Son and the Holy Spirit, and teach them to observe all that I have commanded you. And be assured, I am with you always, to the end of time.'   MATTHEW 28:19-20

The disciples' mission is not narrowly nationalistic, but universal. And Jesus promises that his own presence will no longer be limited by space or time. Always—in all ways and forever—wherever his disciples are, whether it be in a country village, a prison camp, or a city ghetto—Christ will be with them.

The Ascension

The Ascension marks the end of Jesus' visible presence and the beginning of his promised invisible and unlimited presence.

When he had said this, as they watched, he was lifted up, and a cloud removed him from their sight. As he was going, and as they were gazing intently into the sky, all at once there stood beside them two men in white who said, 'Men of Galilee, why stand there looking up into the sky? This Jesus, who has been taken away from you up to heaven, will come in the same way as you have seen him go.'   ACTS 1:9-11

Luke, the author of this account in Acts, is trying to describe a timeless, intangible feeling and experience in terms of a physical event in time. He describes Jesus pictorially as going up, as if heaven were a geographical location high in the sky. Heaven, of course, is not a place, but a state of being: union with God. But it is natural to picture heaven in terms of "upness." We speak of success in school or business in terms of "upness:" "His grades went up," "That man has really gone up in the world." But we know when we say this that success is not a place that is literally up, but a state of being. Jesus could not just slowly fade away. Luke uses pictorial language to try to convey the significance of Jesus' final departure: Jesus—his whole being—is now raised up to union with God. The Ascension has a threefold significance:

1. Christ, God's expression of himself in human form, left behind all privileges in order to enter the inner city of the world, to suffer and die at men's hands. But God raised him from the dead, and he appeared alive and present among his disciples. The Ascension marks the completion of Jesus' earthly life, the end of his visible presence. Christian tradition has referred to the ascended Christ as Victor or King, symbolizing his victory over evil and death and his presence in men's lives (reigning in men's hearts, unlimited by time or space). Christ is not a dead hero whom we remember from the past. He is alive and present in the universe.

2. Jesus ascends as man, fulfilling the true end for which humanity was created: to live and reign with God. He does not leave his humanity, but takes it with him. The Ascension preface to the Sanctus acclaims the Christ "who . . . ascended up into heaven, to prepare a place for us; that where he is, thither we might also ascend, and reign with him in glory" (PB, 78). Christ the perfect man blazes the trail for us to man's final goal: union with and in the being of God.

3. Luke's account concludes: "This Jesus, who has been taken away from you up to heaven, will come in the same way as you have seen him go." J. B. Phillips writes: "history is going somewhere, . . . history is not a mere chance succession of events . . . , there is an ultimate purpose and goal in the universe." That goal is the triumph of justice and love which is symbolized by Christ's coming again to rule on earth. He whose being radiated love, and whom men subjected to the deepest humiliation, is now enthroned and in the end will be victorious. The Ascension, then, asserts nothing less than the ultimate meaningfulness and justice of the universe: the ultimate triumph of good over evil.

The Early
Christian Community

From the earliest times one of the terms men have used to describe God is "Spirit." The Greek word for spirit literally means "wind." "Wind" describes the way God acts. We cannot see the wind itself, but we can see and feel its effects. We can see it blow a piece of paper along a street or bend a leaf on a tree. We cannot see God, but we can feel his presence and see how he affects people's lives. Wind is free —men do not control the way it moves. And, of course, men cannot control God. "Spirit" in Greek also indicates the breath or life which moves people. A team that has spirit can do things in so inspired a way, with its potential so fully realized, that people say "the players outdid themselves," while a team without spirit lives up to none of its potential.

Before the Ascension, Jesus promised that, though he would not be physically present with his disciples, the Spirit of God would guide and inspire them. Jesus speaks of the Spirit of God (or Holy Spirit) as the Paraclete. This Greek word can be translated in a number of ways: as "Advocate" (one who defends the disciples), as "Strengthener" (one who gives them courage), and as "Energizer" (one who inspires them). All are appropriate translations because all speak of an aspect of God's Spirit. It is this Spirit which will guide and instruct the disciples and give them a genuine serenity in the face of opposition.

'If you love me you will obey my commands; and I will ask the Father, and he will give you another to be your Advocate,

who will be with you forever—the Spirit of truth. The world
cannot receive him, because the world neither sees nor knows
him; but you know him, because he dwells with you and is in
you. I will not leave you bereft; I am coming back to you. . . .
I have told you all this while I am still here with you; but your
Advocate, the Holy Spirit whom the Father will send in my
name, will teach you everything, and will call to mind all that
I have told you. Peace is my parting gift to you, my own peace,
such as the world cannot give. Set your troubled hearts at rest,
and banish your fears. You heard me say, "I am going away,
and coming back to you." '   JOHN 14:15-18, 25-28

The peace which men get from the world is the peace
which comes from the avoidance of trouble or the escape
from pain. The peace which Jesus gives is very different.
He promises no escape from suffering. His peace is the serenity of doing what is right regardless of the consequences,
with the knowledge that what happens to one on earth is not
the final chapter in life. The disciples are called to bear
witness to Jesus in spite of the dangers involved.

'But when your Advocate has come, whom I will send you
from the Father—the Spirit of truth that issues from the Father
—he will bear witness to me. And you also are my witnesses,
because you have been with me from the first.'
                                               JOHN 15:26-27

"Witness" translates the Greek word *martyros* which also, in
English, means martyr. Witnessing to Christ in the world
may involve suffering and even death.

'I have told you all this to guard you against the breakdown
of your faith. They will ban you from the synagogue; indeed,
the time is coming when anyone who kills you will suppose
that he is performing a religious duty. They will do these things
because they do not know either the Father or me. I have told
you all this so that when the times comes for it to happen you
may remember my warning.'   JOHN 16:1-4

But God's Spirit will strengthen the disciples in the midst of trouble.

'When you are brought before synagogues and state authorities, do not begin worrying about how you will conduct your defence or what you will say. For when the time comes the Holy Spirit will instruct you what to say.'   LUKE 12:11-12

The Day of Pentecost

In Acts, Luke tells of the fulfillment of Jesus' promise on the day of Pentecost. As usual Luke describes an inward experience as a concrete, colorful, outward event. The Jewish holiday Pentecost commemorated the giving of the law to Moses. The giving of the law (the old law) was accompanied by wind and fire, and Luke describes the giving of the new law (the Spirit of God) in similar terms. The disciples have gathered to celebrate the holiday, probably in the upper room where the Last Supper had taken place.

While the day of Pentecost was running its course they were all together in one place, when suddenly there came from the sky a noise like that of a strong driving wind, which filled the whole house where they were sitting. And there appeared to them tongues like flames of fire, dispersed among them and resting on each one. And they were all filled with the Holy Spirit and began to talk in other tongues, as the Spirit gave them power of utterance. Now there were living in Jerusalem devout Jews drawn from every nation under heaven; and at this sound the crowd gathered, all bewildered because each one heard his own language spoken. They were amazed and in their astonishment exclaimed, 'Why, they are all Galileans, are they not, these men who are speaking? How is it then that we hear them, each of us in his own native language? Parthians, Medes, Elamites; inhabitants of Mesopotamia, of Judaea and Cappadocia, of Pontus and Asia, of Phrygia and Pamphylia, of Egypt and the districts of Libya around Cyrene; visitors from Rome, both Jews and proselytes, Cretans and Arabs, we heard them telling in our own tongues the great things God has done.'   ACTS 2:1-11

Wind is an obvious symbol of the Spirit since both are the same word in Greek. Fire is the symbol of zeal. We call an orator "fiery" if he is particularly zealous and enthusiastic. This is what Luke means when he speaks of "tongues like flames of fire." The "native languages" may be various dialects of the two languages, Aramaic and Greek, which the apostles and all Jews and converts spoke. Luke wants us to realize that the "great things God has done" are for all men regardless of language or race or nationality. It is possible, however, that Luke, a gentile who probably was not present on this occasion, misunderstood the whole incident. Many scholars believe that what really happened was an ecstatic experience of glossolalia, speaking in tongues. This interpretation emphasizes the excitement, enthusiasm, and ecstacy which characterized the early Christian community.

Whatever literally happened, the apostles are obviously exuberant, enthusiastic, and spirited. The crowd's reaction to them is mixed.

And they were all amazed and perplexed, saying to one another, 'What can this mean?' Others said contemptuously, 'They have been drinking!'   ACTS 2:12-13

Peter—who a short time ago had denied Christ and fled in fear—responds to this charge with the first public proclamation of the story of Jesus. Note his emphasis on the Resurrection.

But Peter stood up with the Eleven, raised his voice, and addressed them: 'Fellow Jews, and all you who live in Jerusalem, mark this and give me a hearing. These men are not drunk, as you imagine; for it is only nine in the morning. No, this is what the prophet spoke of: "God says, 'This will happen in the last days: I will pour out upon everyone a portion of my spirit; and your sons and daughters shall prophesy; your young men shall see visions, and your old men shall dream dreams.' "

'Men of Israel, listen to me: I speak of Jesus of Nazareth, a man singled out by God and made known to you through miracles, portents, and signs, which God worked among you through him, as you well know. When he had been given up to you, by the deliberate will and plan of God, you used heathen men to crucify and kill him. But God raised him to life again, setting him free from the pangs of death, because it could not be that death should keep him in its grip. Let all Israel then accept as certain that God has made this Jesus, whom you crucified, both Lord and Messiah.' When they heard this they were cut to the heart, and said to Peter and the apostles, 'Friends, what are we to do?' 'Repent,' said Peter, 'repent and be baptized, every one of you, in the name of Jesus the Messiah for the forgiveness of your sins; and you will receive the gift of the Holy Spirit. For the promise is to you, and to your children, and to all who are far away, everyone whom the Lord our God may call.' In these and many other words he pressed his case and pleaded with them: 'Save yourselves', he said, 'from this crooked age.' Then those who accepted his word were baptized, and some three thousand were added to their number that day.

ACTS 2:14-17, 22-24, 36-41

When a gentile became a Jew, the Jews asked him to undergo a symbolic act of cleansing (baptism means "washing"). Peter suggests to the Jews that they undergo this same symbolic washing as a sign of their repentance and of their desire to lead a new life.

The Early Christian Community in Jerusalem

The disciples have been transformed by a series of dramatic experiences: the risen Christ's presence, his ascension, and the awareness of the presence of the Spirit in their lives. Emotional experiences and visions are not uncommon, but it is very difficult to know whether they are genuine or fraudulent and delusional. The best way to test the validity of such experiences is to observe whether in the long run they bear fruit in the lives of those who claim them. We all know people who "get religion" one day, and a week later they have forgotten all about it and have become the same old persons. Luke's description of the early Christian community shows a group who "got religion" and kept it. Their experience led in the long run to acts of courage and love.

Though they differed from ordinary Jews in regarding Jesus as the Messiah, the first Christians continued to live in Jerusalem. They kept all the Jewish customs, and differed from their fellow Jews in only three ways: they formed their own synagogues (the local congregation to which Jews belonged in addition to the Temple of Jerusalem), they celebrated the Lord's Supper on Sunday, and they held property in common.

They met constantly to hear the apostles teach, and to share the common life, to break bread, and to pray. A sense of awe was everywhere, and many marvels and signs were brought about through the apostles. All whose faith had drawn them together held everything in common: they would sell their property and possessions and make a general distribution as the need of each required. With one mind they kept up their daily attendance at the temple, and, breaking bread in private houses, shared their meals with unaffected joy, as they praised God and enjoyed the favour of the whole people. And day by day the Lord added to their number those whom he was saving.   ACTS 2:42-47

An exuberance characterized everything undertaken by this community. They flung themselves into a communistic economic experiment which eventually proved unrealistic. Their

gatherings were so unabashedly joyful that the Jewish
leaders charged them with being frivolous. Peter and John
spoke with such candor and ardor that they were constantly
hauled before judges and courts.

So they brought them and stood them before the Council;
and the High Priest began his examination. 'We expressly
ordered you', he said, 'to desist from teaching in that name;
and what has happened? You have filled Jerusalem with your
teaching, and you are trying to make us responsible for that
man's death.' Peter replied for himself and the apostles: 'We
must obey God rather than men. The God of our fathers raised
up Jesus whom you had done to death by hanging him on a
gibbet. He it is whom God has exalted with his own right hand
as leader and saviour, to grant Israel repentance and forgiveness of sins. And we are witnesses to all this, and so is the
Holy Spirit given by God to those who are obedient to him.'

ACTS 5:27-32

The Martyrdom of Stephen

The Jewish leaders naturally resented the Christian claims
and feared the damage this splinter group might do. The
Christian community, however, was not intimidated by their
warnings. One of the Christian Jews, the Greek-speaking
Stephen, especially roused their anger by telling them that,
by their actions, they had forfeited their right to be called
the chosen people.

'How stubborn you are, heathen still at heart and deaf to the
truth! You always fight against the Holy Spirit. Like fathers, like
sons. Was there ever a prophet whom your fathers did not
persecute? They killed those who foretold the coming of the
Righteous One; and now you have betrayed him and murdered
him, you who received the Law as God's angels gave it to you,
and yet have not kept it.' This touched them on the raw and
they ground their teeth with fury. But Stephen, filled with the

Holy Spirit, and gazing intently up to heaven, saw the glory of God, and Jesus standing at God's right hand. 'Look,' he said, 'there is a rift in the sky; I can see the Son of Man standing at God's right hand!' At this they gave a great shout and stopped their ears. Then they made one rush at him and, flinging him out of the city, set about stoning him. The witnesses laid their coats at the feet of a young man named Saul. So they stoned Stephen, and as they did so, he called out, 'Lord Jesus, receive my spirit.' Then he fell on his knees and cried aloud, 'Lord, do not hold this sin against them', and with that he died. And Saul was among those who approved his murder.   ACTS 7:51-8:1

Saul (better known by his Roman name Paul) was among the religious leaders who stood by while Stephen was lynched without trial. Stephen dies echoing Christ's words of forgiveness. He is the first Christian martyr, the first to witness to Christ with his life. Note that Luke, in telling about Stephen, describes him as filled with the Holy Spirit. There are some who think that "filled with the Holy Spirit" should mean a nice warm glow of spiritual satisfaction. Stephen's death is a better indication of what it means to let God's Spirit enter our lives. The Spirit did not lead Stephen to comfort, but to danger and death. Stephen's death marks the beginning of a long era of persecution in which the genuineness of the Christian community's commitment will be severely tested.

Paul—Apostle to the Gentiles

Though we first meet Saul of Tarsus in Acts (in Luke's description of his participation in the stoning of Stephen), as Paul he was to become the man most responsible for the transformation of Christianity from a small Jewish sect into a worldwide religion.

Paul's background made him uniquely qualified to be the organizer of Christianity's worldwide mission. Five hundred years before he was born, many of the Jewish people had left Israel to settle in small groups in cities throughout the Mediterranean area. Though these Jews had contacts with the people of the cities within which they settled, they nonetheless preserved their Jewish identity. Paul was born into a strict Pharisaic Jewish family in Tarsus, a city in Asia Minor. He studied to be a rabbi under the great Jewish scholar Gamaliel in Jerusalem. He proved himself a brilliant pupil and quickly emerged as one of the most influential young men in the Jewish community. Living in Tarsus, he, of necessity, came into contact with non-Jews. Tarsus was a cosmopolitan Greek-speaking city. It was not only a leading trade center, but its university made it one of the world's great intellectual centers. The literature and philosophy of Greece and Rome were therefore not unfamiliar to Paul. He also had another rare advantage; he possessed what few outside Italy, gentile or Jew, were privileged to have: Roman citizenship, inherited from his father. This gave him not only stature but the protection of the Roman Emperor.

Luke, his companion, gives us a good picture of Paul. Short, bald, and hooknosed, he had sharp eyes with shaggy eyebrows. Intensity perhaps best describes his personality. Whatever he decided to undertake, he pursued to the fullest extent. He was not always patient with the partial commitment of others and could be bitter and angry when thwarted.

Paul's great cause as a young man was the suppression of the Christian menace. Paul, as a sophisticated Jew, regarded the Christians as uneducated fanatics who were subverting Judaism by declaring that an ignorant peasant, Jesus of Nazareth, was the Messiah. And he was especially infuriated by the Greek-speaking Jews, such as Stephen, who became Christians and denounced the Jewish leaders for killing Christ.

The Conversion

After Stephen's stoning, Paul set out for Damascus, with the official license of the Jewish hierarchy, to persecute the growing Christian community there. On the road to Damascus, however, Paul's outlook was utterly transformed. Many years later, when he was on trial for his life, he described what happened.

'I am a true-born Jew,' he said, 'a native of Tarsus in Cilicia. I was brought up in this city, and as a pupil of Gamaliel I was thoroughly trained in every point of our ancestral law. I have always been ardent in God's service, as you all are today. And so I began to persecute this movement to the death, arresting its followers, men and women alike, and putting them in chains. For this I have as witnesses the High Priest and the whole Council of Elders. I was given letters from them to our fellow-Jews at Damascus, and had started out to bring the Christians there to Jerusalem as prisoners for punishment; and this is what happened. I was on the road and nearing Damascus, when suddenly about midday a great light flashed from the sky all around me, and I fell to the ground. Then I heard a voice saying to me, "Saul, Saul, why do you persecute me?" I answered, "Tell me, Lord, who you are." "I am Jesus of Nazareth," he said, "whom you are persecuting." My companions saw the light, but did not hear the voice that spoke to me. "What shall I do, Lord?" I said, and the Lord replied, "Get up and continue your journey to Damascus; there you will be told of all the tasks that are laid upon you." As I had been blinded by the brilliance of that light, my companions led me by the hand, and so I came to Damascus.

'There, a man called Ananias, a devout observer of the Law and well spoken of by all the Jews of that place, came and stood beside me and said, "Saul, my brother, recover your sight." Instantly I recovered my sight and saw him. He went on: "The God of our fathers appointed you to know his will and to see the Righteous One and to hear his very voice, because you are to be his witness before the world, and testify to what you have seen and heard. And now why delay? Be baptized at once, with invocation of his name, and wash away your sins." '

ACTS 22:3-16

Every school child has had the experience, in trying to find the answer to a math problem, of spending a long time pursuing a fruitless approach only suddenly to "see the light." On a much vaster scale, this was Paul's experience. We do not know what led to his dramatic change. Perhaps Stephen's brave serenity in the face of death left an impression on him which he could not forget. Perhaps he had grown more and more disillusioned with the superficiality of the law and its failure to motivate goodness. We only know for sure that this incident on the road to Damascus utterly transformed Paul. He set out to destroy Christianity, breathing threats, and he arrived in Damascus blinded and shattered, believing he had met Christ. The community he set out to destroy now received him as a member.

After his conversion (in about A.D. 32) Paul went alone into the Arabian desert. This period of solitude served the same purpose as Christ's temptation in the wilderness after his baptism; and he returned to Damascus certain of his calling to be a follower of Jesus. His preaching in Damascus was so brilliantly incisive that the Jewish leaders plotted to kill him.

As the days mounted up, the Jews hatched a plot against his life; but their plans became known to Saul. They kept watch on the city gates day and night so that they might murder him; but his converts took him one night and let him down by the wall, lowering him in a basket.   ACTS 9:23-25

Paul then journeyed to Jerusalem where he was naturally regarded with hostile suspicion by the Christian community he had previously persecuted. Only Barnabas was friendly. Paul soon returned to his home town of Tarsus where he remained for eight years. Here he appears to have tried to demonstrate the genuineness of his Christian commitment by working quietly among the gentiles.

Apostle to the Gentiles

About a year after the Resurrection, a sizeable group of Jewish Christians migrated from Jerusalem to Antioch. In Antioch they began the practice of admitting gentiles (non-Jews) into the Christian community. The Jerusalem Christians (who continued to strictly obey all the Jewish laws) were upset by this action and sent Barnabas to investigate. Barnabas was so favorably impressed that he stayed and persuaded Paul to come from Tarsus and work with him.

In A.D. 45—whether through natural disaster or because of the inefficiency of their economic practices—the Jerusalem Christians were afflicted by famine. This gave Barnabas and Paul a natural opportunity to return there (bringing money collected from Antioch Christians) and to explain their favorable impression of the practices of the Antioch Church.

The apostles Peter and John agreed that Paul and Barnabas should be permitted to proclaim Christianity to the gentiles, while Peter and John would be responsible for the conversion of Jews. They all shook hands in public as a sign of agreement.

Paul and Barnabas then set out on their first missionary journey to the gentiles (A.D. 47–48). The journey was full of wild adventures: they fell into bitter controversies with the Jews again and again; their deaths were plotted several times, and Paul was stoned and presumed dead. When they returned to Antioch they walked directly into another crisis. Some of the Jerusalem Christians, apparently going back on the previous agreement, had come to Antioch in their absence and stirred up trouble by saying that any gentile who wanted to be a Christian must first become a Jew. Paul and Barnabas angrily denied this, of course, and said gentile converts had neither to obey the intricate Jewish dietary laws nor receive the Jewish initiation rite of circumcision. Fierce dissension broke out, and Paul and Barnabas finally went to Jerusalem again to protest to the apostles and to rebuke them for going back on their word. This meeting, known as the Council of Jerusalem, took place in A.D. 49.

When they reached Jerusalem they were welcomed by the church and the apostles and elders, and reported all that God had done through them. Then some of the Pharisaic party who had become believers came forward and said, 'They must be circumcised and told to keep the Law of Moses.' The apostles and elders held a meeting to look into this matter; and, after a long debate, Peter rose and addressed them. 'My friends,' he said, 'in the early days, as you yourselves know, God made his choice among you and ordained that from my lips the Gentiles should hear and believe the message of the Gospel. And God, who can read men's minds, showed his approval of them by giving the Holy Spirit to them, as he did to us. He made no difference between them and us; for he purified their hearts by faith. Then why do you now provoke God by laying on the shoulders of these converts a yoke which neither we nor our fathers were able to bear? No, we believe that it is by the grace of the Lord Jesus that we are saved, and so are they.' At that the whole company fell silent and listened to Barnabas and Paul as they told of all the signs and miracles that God had worked among the Gentiles through them.   ACTS 15:4-12

Paul and Barnabas reminded the apostles and elders that God was the father of all and that Christ had lived and died not just for the Jews, but for all men. Paul and Barnabas prevailed, and the whole body agreed to send out a general letter stating that gentiles need not become Jews in order to be Christians. All that was asked was that gentiles avoid immoralities offensive to the Jews.

'We the apostles and elders, send greetings as brothers to our brothers of gentile origin in Antioch, Syria, and Cilicia. Forasmuch as we have heard that some of our number, without any instructions from us, have disturbed you with their talk and unsettled your minds, we have resolved unanimously to send to you our chosen representatives with our well-beloved Barnabas and Paul, who have devoted themselves to the cause of our Lord Jesus Christ. We are therefore sending Judas and Silas, who will themselves confirm this by word of mouth. It is the decision of the Holy Spirit, and our decision, to lay no further burden upon you beyond these essentials: you are to abstain from meat that has been offered to idols, from blood, from anything that has been strangled, and from fornication. If you keep yourselves free from these things you will be doing right. Farewell.'   ACTS 15:23-29

The Jerusalem Council, the first of many councils of the leaders of the Church, established the conciliar method as the means by which the Church throughout its history would decide controversial questions. Decisions were to be made not by one leader claiming full authority, but by all the

Church's leaders together after they had discussed the issues.

The Council of Jerusalem ended the attempt to keep Christianity a small racial-nationalistic Jewish sect. Paul was now licensed as Apostle to the Gentiles, and Christianity burst the confines of Judaism to become worldwide. Following the pattern of his earlier trip with Barnabas, Paul now undertook a second and third missionary journey (A.D. 49–52 and A.D. 52–56) in which he visited nearly every major city of the Mediterranean world, establishing and encouraging Christian communities in each. In Luke's vivid account of these journeys in Acts, we see Paul almost constantly in controversy, riot, persecution, and danger of death. On the other hand Paul had many advantages. World conditions were extraordinarily favorable for his endeavor. Roman dominance of the world had ushered in one of the longest periods of peace in history. The straight roads which the Romans built everywhere (for military purposes) made travel easy, and the fact that nearly everyone spoke one of the two common languages (Greek and Latin) facilitated communication.

Paul's Message

Not only was Paul the early Church's most eloquent preacher, but also his epistles (letters) to Christian congregations in various cities are the earliest Christian writings and make up a quarter of the New Testament. The message of both his letters and sermons is the same: acceptance of God's love as revealed in Christ can transform men's lives.

As a young man Paul had attempted to live strictly by the Jewish law. He shared his fellow Jews' belief that they were God's chosen people and that to remain in a right relationship with God it was necessary only to obey the law. Jewish religion had become for many the formalized practice of complex regulations. But as time went on, Paul grew progressively disenchanted with this kind of legalistic Judaism.

Though the law might in some ways be a helpful guide and standard, it could not motivate men to do good, but rather reminded them of what was evil.

> For (again from Scripture) 'no human being can be justified in the sight of God' for having kept the law: law brings only the consciousness of sin.   ROMANS 3:20

At the same time that he was growing disenchanted with the Jewish law's ability to change men, his persecution of the Christians brought him into contact with people such as Stephen whose lives had been transformed by commitment to a person. Then, of course, on the road to Damascus Paul felt himself overwhelmed by that person, and his life was utterly changed.

Paul's recurring theme is that "man is justified by God's grace received through faith in Christ." "Justification" is the technical term Paul uses to describe man's right relationship with God. We are not, in Paul's view, justified by keeping the law. Men cannot earn God's favor by doing particular outward acts. God's love is freely given, and we see this freely-given love most clearly in Christ. All we need do is to accept that love, to unite ourselves with Christ and enter upon a new way of life.

> When anyone is united to Christ, there is a new world; the old order has gone, and a new order has already begun. From first to last this has been the work of God. He has reconciled us men to himself through Christ, and he has enlisted us in this service of reconcilation. What I mean is, that God was in Christ reconciling the world to himself.   2 CORINTHIANS 5:17-19

Paul calls God's freely-given love, portrayed in Christ, "grace." We are then saved not by what we do, but by God's grace, which we receive by accepting it ("faith in Christ").

For all alike have sinned, and are deprived of the divine splendour, and all are justified by God's free grace alone, through his act of liberation in the person of Christ Jesus. For God designed him to be the means of expiating sin by his sacrificial death, effective through faith. God meant by this to demonstrate his justice, because in his forbearance he had overlooked the sins of the past—to demonstrate his justice now in the present, showing that he is both himself just and justifies any man who puts his faith in Jesus. What room then is left for human pride? It is excluded. And on what principle? The keeping of the law would not exclude it, but faith does. For our argument is that a man is justified by faith quite apart from success in keeping the law.   ROMANS 3:23-28

If we accept God's freely-given love, we enter upon a new life. Paul describes this as "life in Christ" or "life in the Spirit." It is life lived in a wholly new dimension.

Those who live on the level of our lower nature have their outlook formed by it, and that spells death; but those who live on the level of the spirit have the spiritual outlook, and that is life and peace. For the outlook of the lower nature is enmity with God; it is not subject to the law of God; indeed it cannot be: those who live on such a level cannot possibly please God. But that is now how you live. You are on the spiritual level, if only God's Spirit dwells within you; and if a man does not possess the Spirit of Christ, he is no Christian. But if Christ is dwelling within you, then although the body is a dead thing because you sinned, yet the spirit is life itself because you have been justified.   ROMANS 8:5-10

Those who "live in Christ" are nothing less than God's sons and, along with Christ, can address God in the most intimate way as "Abba."

For all who are moved by the Spirit of God are sons of God. The Spirit you have received is not a spirit of slavery leading you back into a life of fear, but a Spirit that makes us sons, enabling us to cry "Abba! Father!" In that cry the Spirit of God joins with our spirit in testifying that we are God's children; and if children, then heirs. We are God's heirs and Christ's fellow-heirs, if we share his sufferings now in order to share his splendour hereafter.   ROMANS 8:14-17

All the good things which the law tried formally to compel men to do, are now natural to those who accept their calling to be God's sons.

What the law could never do, because our lower nature robbed it of all potency, God has done: by sending his own Son in a form like that of our own sinful nature, and as a sacrifice for sin, he has passed judgement against sin within that very nature, so that the commandment of the law may find fulfilment in us, whose conduct, no longer under the control of our lower nature, is directed by the Spirit.   ROMANS 8:3-4

The conclusion of Paul's message is invariably the same. Having unfolded the glorious possibility of new life "in Christ," he urges men to commitment.

Therefore, my brothers, I implore you by God's mercy to offer your very selves to him: a living sacrifice, dedicated and fit for his acceptance, the worship offered by mind and heart. Adapt yourselves no longer to the pattern of this present world, but let your minds be remade and your whole nature thus transformed.   ROMANS 12:1-2

Imprisonment and Death

Being led by the Spirit to realize our calling as sons of God does not produce a cozy feeling of security. Rather it can lead a person into the kind of sacrifice that was demanded of Christ. Under attack, Paul writes to the Corinthian church of the dangers he has had to face as Christ's apostle, dangers that would have killed most men.

But if there is to be bravado (and here I speak as a fool), I can indulge in it too. Are they Hebrews? So am I. Israelites? So am I. Abraham's desendants? So am I. Are they servants of Christ? I am mad to speak like this, but I can outdo them. More overworked than they, scourged more severely, more often imprisoned, many a time face to face with death. Five times the Jews have given me the thirty-nine strokes; three times I have been beaten with rods; once I was stoned; three times I have been shipwrecked, and for twenty-four hours I was adrift on the open sea. I have been constantly on the road; I have met dangers from rivers, dangers from robbers, dangers from my fellow-countrymen, dangers from foreigners, dangers in towns, dangers in the country, dangers at sea, dangers from false friends. I have toiled and drudged, I have often gone without sleep; hungry and thirsty, I have often gone fasting; and I have suffered from cold and exposure. Apart from these external things, there is the responsibility that weighs on me every day, my anxious concern for all our congregations. If anyone is weak, do I not share his weakness? If anyone is made to stumble, does my heart not blaze with indignation? If boasting there must be, I will boast of the things that show up my weakness.   2 CORINTHIANS 11:21-30

In A.D. 56 Paul again took money to the Christians in Jerusalem suffering financial hardships. While he was there the Jews had him arrested. His presence caused such rioting and clamor that Paul had to be smuggled out of the city for a hearing at Caesaria to the south. After two years in prison there, his appeal, as a Roman citizen, to the emperor was honored, and he was sent to Rome for trial. After a hair-raising journey and shipwreck, he finally arrived in the capital city in A.D. 59. Though he was allowed limited freedom as he awaited trial, it was nonetheless a time of hardship and disappointment. In the year 64, as he sensed his life was about to be taken, he wrote to his friend Timothy.

As for me, already my life is being poured out on the altar, and the hour for my departure is upon me. I have run the great

race, I have finished the course, I have kept faith. Do your best
to join me soon; for Demas has deserted me because his heart
was set on this world; he has gone to Thessalonica, Crescens
to Galatia, Titus to Dalmatia; I have no one with me but Luke.
At the first hearing of my case no one came into court to
support me; they all left me in the lurch. But the Lord stood
by me and lent me strength, so that I might be his instrument
in making the full proclamation of the Gospel for the whole
pagan world to hear; and thus I was rescued out of the lion's
jaws. And the Lord will rescue me from every attempt to do
me harm, and keep me safe until his heavenly reign begins.
Glory to him for ever and ever! Amen.

2 TIMOTHY 4:6-7, 9-11, 16-18

The New Testament tells us nothing about Paul's death.
The most substantial body of evidence outside the Bible indicates that he was beheaded in Rome, probably in the Emperor Nero's persecution in A.D. 64.

At the time of his death, flourishing Christian communities
existed in almost every city of the Roman Empire. Opposed
at every turn, threatened, beaten, left for dead, disgraced,
imprisoned, Paul never lost courage. He regarded himself as
armed with the "sword of the Spirit," the conviction that no
matter what men did to him in earthly life, in the end "all
things work together for good for those who give their lives
to God."

With all this in mind, what are we to say? If God is on our
side, who is against us? He did not spare his own Son, but
surrendered him for us all; and with this gift how can he fail
to lavish upon us all he has to give? Who will be the accuser
of God's chosen ones? It is God who pronounces acquittal;
then who can condemn? It is Christ—Christ who died, and,
more than that, was raised from the dead—who is at God's
right hand, and indeed pleads our cause. Then what can separate us from the love of Christ? Can affliction or hardship? Can
persecution, hunger, nakedness, peril, or the sword? 'We are

being done to death for thy sake all day long,' as Scripture says; 'we have been treated like sheep for slaughter'—and yet, in spite of all, overwhelming victory is ours through him who loved us. For I am convinced that there is nothing in death or life, in the realm of spirits or superhuman powers, in the world as it is or the world as it shall be, in the forces of the universe, in heights or depths—nothing in all creation that can separate us from the love of God in Christ Jesus our Lord.

ROMANS 8:31-39

Persecution

20

The Church developed in the same way a human being does. As a child grows older, though he remains the same person, he undergoes changes in appearance and outlook. As Christianity expanded from a handful of Jewish peasants into a worldwide body of hundreds of thousands, the early informality naturally gave way to a more formal sort of structure.

The Growth of the Church

ORGANIZATION

A three-fold order of ordained ministers developed as leaders and servants of the Christian community:

Bishops. Jesus chose twelve as the apostles. Mark writes: "He appointed twelve as his companions, whom he would send out to proclaim the Gospel." After his death the apostles were naturally the nucleus of the Christian community. They were "overseers" ("bishops") of congregations. As they grew older, and as the number of congregations increased, the apostles passed on the leadership duties Christ had given them to men they chose or to men chosen by the local congregations. They transmitted this commission as "overseer" by laying their hands on the head of the person chosen. Bishops today receive their office from other bishops who are links in an unbroken chain that stretches back to the apostles, a chain called "the Apostolic Succession." Bishops today usually are leaders of a number of Christian communities (parishes) in some geographical subdivision, such as Chicago or

Utah. In addition to their role as overseers, bishops have two special sacramental functions: to confirm and to ordain.

Priests. The men the apostles first chose to oversee new congregations were also called "elders" ("presbyters" in Greek). But as the Church expanded, the title "elder" came to describe the leader of a single congregation, and only a few elders held the title "overseer." The bishop's function then became the overseeing of groups of local congregations. Presbyters came to be commonly called "priests." The title "minister" (which means "servant") properly refers to all Christ's followers. Confirmation is the commissioning of men and women as ministers. The priest's calling is to be a minister to ministers. His special function is preaching and teaching and celebrating the Lord's Supper for the community.

Deacons. As the number of Christians increased, the apostles found themselves so bogged down in the details of administration, waiting on table, visiting the sick, and helping the poor, that they set aside certain men as deacons (which also means "servants") who could help with these tasks. Luke records the ordination of the first deacons.

During this period, when disciples were growing in number, there was disagreement between those of them who spoke Greek and those who spoke the language of the Jews. The former party complained that their widows were being overlooked in the daily distribution. So the Twelve called the whole body of disciples together and said, 'It would be a grave mistake for us to neglect the word of God in order to wait at table. Therefore, friends, look out seven men of good reputation from your number, men full of the Spirit and of wisdom, and we will appoint them to deal with these matters, while we devote ourselves to prayer and to the ministry of the Word.' This proposal proved acceptable to the whole body. They elected Stephen, a man full of faith and of the Holy Spirit, Philip, Prochorus, Nicanor, Timon, Parmenas, and Nicolas of Antioch, a former convert to Judaism. These they pre-

sented to the apostles, who prayed and laid their hands on
them.   ACTS 6:1-6

Today, before becoming a priest, a man must serve at least
six months as a deacon. And though he may become a priest
or bishop, he remains forever a deacon as well. This reminds
him that his first duty as an ordained minister is always to
render service, even of the most menial sort. The three-fold
order of leadership functioned so satisfactorily that it was not
challenged until the Protestant Reformation when splinter
groups of Christians tried other forms of organization. In
most of the Christian Church today, the threefold leadership
continues, and there are indications that some branches of
the Church with different leadership structures will return
to the original practice.

WORSHIP AND FELLOWSHIP

The Christians were persecuted first by some of their fellow Jews and then by the Romans. They therefore met—
often secretly—in houses. Christians in a given area were
almost a family. Central to their lives was the gathering on
Sunday for the Lord's Supper. In the earliest days this took
place in the midst of their meals together. At these meals
some expressed their love for one another so avidly that St.
Paul was compelled to rebuke them. He reminded the Corinthian Christians that the worship of the community should
take place "decently and in order." Great care was taken
over the initiation of new members into the community.
Baptism—a symbolic washing away of the old life—was administered only after lengthy instruction and a personal
pledge of commitment to Christ by the candidate.

THE SCRIPTURES

The story of Jesus was spread by word of mouth. The
earliest written records are the letters ("epistles") which
Paul wrote the churches he founded. These letters, often

written in haste, focus mainly on Christ's passion, death, and resurrection; they contain almost nothing about his life and teachings.

Only when those who had known Jesus began to die did the Christian community see the need to write down the disciples' recollections. The earliest collection of Jesus' teachings was made at Antioch about A.D. 50 by an unknown person. It is known as "Q" (after the German word *quelle*, "source"). Another source, Mark's Gospel, is usually associated with Mark, the nephew of Barnabas and a close associate of Peter. Written about A.D. 65, Mark's Gospel is a skeletal chronological narrative of Jesus' life. About A.D. 80, Luke, a Greek doctor close to Paul, along with an unknown author who was probably close to Matthew the Apostle, wrote accounts of Jesus' life. They both made use of Q and Mark. But both also referred to other sources, oral and written, and so both recount incidents in Jesus' life not found in Q or Mark. About A.D. 100, John the Elder, who was close to John the Apostle (Christ's closest friend), wrote down John's reflections and tried to explain Christ's significance in terms of Greek philosophy. John's Gospel is thus a mixture of vivid first-hand memories and Jewish and Greek philosophical thought. Because Matthew and Luke both made use of Mark and Q, the Gospels of Matthew, Mark, and Luke are called "synoptic" ("seen through the same eyes"). John makes no use of Mark or Q, and in his Gospel we see Christ through different eyes.

As time went on, legends about Jesus arose and were written down. This happens to all great people: there are legends in American folklore about George Washington (cutting down the cherry tree) and Abe Lincoln (studying by the light of the fire). Stories spread about the child Jesus making clay birds which became alive and flew away, and about Jesus lengthening a piece of wood which his father had cut too short. These stories were written down and circulated, but their imaginative and fantastic character and their cloudy origins made them suspect by most who heard or read them. About A.D. 200, the books which now constitute our New Testament had emerged as the accepted and authentic ("canonical") books, though not until 382 did a council of the Church pronounce them the official records.

The Church and the Roman Empire

Roman religion was a formality. Public prayers to the old Roman gods were part of formal state occasions and a sign of loyalty to the empire. Roman officials did not care what gods the various people they ruled worshipped as long as they showed respect for the Roman gods as well as their own. This could be done merely by annually throwing a little incense on the altar of the emperor. The Jews alone, whose belief in one God made such a thing impossible, were allowed to pray *for* the emperor rather than to him.

For a time, the Romans considered Christianity to be a branch of Judaism and left it undisturbed. But the Jewish leaders, bitterly resentful of Christianity's growth, soon urged Roman officials to suppress the movement, declaring it was not part of Judaism. Non-Jewish converts to Christianity also raised the patriotic anger of the Romans by refusing to make the formal sacrifice to the Roman gods and emperor. Christians therefore became suspect as subversives within the empire. Their refusal to worship the Roman gods earned them accusations of atheism. And their claim that Christ was "the way" brought accusations of intolerance.

In A.D. 64 the Roman populace accused the hated Emperor Nero of setting fire to the city of Rome. Needing a scapegoat, Nero blamed the Christians for the fire. Thousands died in the resulting persecution, including (it is most likely) Peter and Paul. The Roman historian Tacitus describes the persecution this way:

But all the emperor's wealth and the propitiations of the gods did not suffice to allay the scandal or banish the belief that the fire had been ordered (by him). And so to get rid of this rumor, Nero set up as the culprits and punished with the utmost refinement of cruelty a class hated for their abominations, who are commonly called Christians. Christus, from whom their name is derived, was executed at the hands of the procurator Pontius Pilate in the reign of Tiberius. Checked for the moment, this pernicious superstition again broke out, not only in Judaea, the source of the evil, but even in Rome, that receptacle for everything that is sordid and degrading from every quarter of the globe, which there finds a following. Accordingly, arrest was first made of those who confessed [to being Christians]. Besides being put to death they were made to serve as objects of amusement; they were clad in the hides of beasts and torn to death by dogs; others were crucified, others set on fire to serve to illuminate the night when daylight failed. Nero had thrown open his grounds for the display, and was putting on a show in the circus where he mingled with the people in the dress of charioteer or drove about in his chariot. All this gave rise to a feeling of pity, even towards men whose guilt merited the most exemplary punishment; for it was felt that they were being destroyed not for the public good but to gratify the cruelty of an individual.   TACITUS, *Annals* 45:44

This was only the beginning. Two hundred and fifty years of persecutions followed in which Christians were tortured or put to death. Marcion records what happened in Smyrna in 155 at the annual festival in honor of the emperor. A number of Christians had been thrown to wild animals in the arena, and the crowd began to cry for the blood of Polycarp (then Bishop of Smyrna). The Roman official tries to persuade Polycarp to swear allegiance to Fortuna, the emperor's goddess protector.

When the proconsul pressed him further and said, "Swear and I set you free: Curse Christ." Polycarp answered, "Eighty-six years have I served Him, and He did me no wrong. How can I blaspheme my King who has saved me?" When the proconsul persevered, saying: "Swear by the Fortune of Caesar," Polycarp answered: "If you vainly imagine that I shall swear by the Fortune of Caesar, as you say, and suppose that I know not what I am, hear a plain answer, 'I am a Christian.' If you wish to learn the Christian's reason, give me a day and listen."

The proconsul said: "I have beasts, and to them I will throw you, unless you change your mind." "Bring them in," Polycarp answered. Again the proconsul spoke to him: "If you don't fear the beasts, I will have you consumed by fire, unless you change your mind." "You threaten me," answered Polycarp, "with the fire that burns for an hour and then goes out. You know nothing of the fire of the judgment to come and eternal punishment which is reserved for the wicked. Why this delay? Bring on what you will."

The proconsul was amazed and sent his own herald to proclaim three times in the midst of the stadium, "Polycarp has admitted that he is a Christian." Upon this proclamation of the herald the whole multitude who were in Smyrna cried aloud in ungovernable fury: "This is the teacher of Asia, the father of the Christians, the destroyer of our Gods, who teaches many not to sacrifice or worship." So saying, they shouted, beseeching Philip the Asiarch to let loose a lion on Polycarp. However, he said it was not lawful for him to do this, and that the wild beasts had already been withdrawn.

Then the crowd cried with one voice that Polycarp should be burnt alive. This was sooner brought about than we can relate. Everyone rushed to gather wood and fuel from shops and baths. When the pyre was ready, Polycarp laid aside his garments, loosened his loin cloth, and took off his shoes. Immediately they stacked the fuel about him, but when they made ready to nail him to the stake as well, he said: "Let me be as I am, for he who has appointed me to suffer by fire will give me also the strength to stand fast in the flames without the help of your nails."

So they bound him without nailing him. And he, with his hands bound behind him, looked up to heaven and said: "Lord

God Almighty, Father of Thy well-beloved and blessed Son, Jesus Christ, through whom we have received the knowledge of Thee, I bless Thee that Thou didst deem me worthy of this day and hour, that I should take a part among the number of the martyrs in the cup of Thy Christ to the resurrection of Life eternal, among whom may I be accepted before Thee today, a rich and acceptable sacrifice, as Thou didst foreordain and foreshow and fulfil, God faithful and true."

A Letter of the Church of Smyrna

A few years later, in 161, the noblest of emperors, Marcus Aurelius, came to power. A philosopher, deeply religious, blameless in his own life, he ruled entirely with the interests of the people in mind. Unfortunately, however, he felt that only by restoring the old Roman religion in its original purity could the empire be strong and the people happy. He therefore tried systematically to erase the "Christian superstition" in the greatest of all persecutions. Like all the others, this persecution served only to unite Christians all the more and to increase their zeal. The Christian theologian Tertullian (160-220) wrote shortly after this persecution, "Kill us, torture us, condemn us, grind us to pieces. The more you mow us down, the more we grow. The blood of martyrs is seed."

Several chaotic reigns followed Marcus Aurelius', and Christians were largely unmolested. Then in 284 the brilliant administrator Diocletian came to power. In 303, in the last persecution, he set out to destroy Christianity once and for all. Clergy were arrested, Christian buildings razed to the ground, and Scriptures burnt. Christians were deprived of all civil rights, and many were executed. But once again persecution apparently served to strengthen the Church.

The Legalization of Christianity

Diocletian had divided the empire into eastern and western parts. After his retirement in 305 a struggle for control

of the western part developed between Constantine and
Maxentius. Constantine's forces were outnumbered and he
was eager for divine help. Eusebius records what happened,
exactly as Constantine told him.

Accordingly [Constantine told me] he began to pray earnestly that God would make himself known to him and in this
immediate need stretch out the right hand of help. While he
was thus engaged there appeared to him a wonderful sign sent
by God. He said that early in the afternoon, when the sun was
past its zenith, he saw in the sky the trophy of a cross, composed of light, standing above the sun. He swore that he saw it
with his own eyes, and that it bore this inscription: "By this
you shall conquer!" He and his whole army—for he was out on
some expedition—likewise witnesses to the miracle, were utterly amazed.

He admitted that he began to doubt within himself concerning the meaning of this apparition. He was still pondering in
his mind when night fell. While he slept the Christ of God
appeared with the same sign that he had been shown in the
sky, and he commanded him to have a standard made in the
same form, and to use it as a protection in battle. He rose very
early and revealed all this to his friends. Then he collected
together craftsmen in gold and precious stones and, sitting
down in the middle, painted as it were a picture in words of
the sign that he had seen, ordering its likeness to be made in
gold and precious stones.

It was composed after this manner. A long spear, plated with
gold, was given a transverse arm to make the form of a cross.
At the top of the spear was fixed a crown of gold and precious
stones. On this was placed the badge of our salvation, that is
to say, the first two letters of the name Christ, Chi and Rho,
the X intersecting the P in the middle, ☧ . Afterwards the Emperor used to wear this monogram on his helmet.

EUSEBIUS, *Life of Constantine,* I:26f.

Constantine defeated Maxentius at the Battle of Milvian
Bridge in 312. After his victory, he did not forget the Chris-

tians. By the Edict of Milan in 313, Constantine, together with the eastern emperor, declared Christianity legal.

Whether Constantine himself became a Christian at once is unclear. When he got control (in 323) of the eastern half of the empire, he realized that Christianity might be a useful unifying force to hold the empire together. He seems gradually to have come to a personal commitment as well. Though he was not baptized until just before his death in 337, his policies show Christian influence. He humanized the criminal law, abolished gladiatorial shows, made grants to support poor children, bettered the condition of slaves (who for years had knelt as equals with the free at the Christian Lord's Supper), had his children reared as Christians, personally built many churches, and made Sunday a public holiday.

Christianity under Constantine became the favored religion of the empire. Though Constantine's nephew, the Emperor Julian (361-363), tried to overthrow Christianity and replace it with the old Roman religion, his effort was a failure. When he died in battle his last words were, "Vixisti Galilaee!" ("Galilean, you have conquered"). The followers of Christ had grown from a tiny group of Jewish peasants into a mighty army that, despite scorn and persecution, finally prevailed: the Christ who had been killed by imperial order was accepted as Lord by him who occupied the imperial throne.

The end of the persecutions was a mixed blessing. As Christianity became more and more the favored and official religion, many persons joined the Church to gain favor with the emperor or because it was the fashionable thing to do. It is sometimes said that Constantine's conversion was the greatest disaster ever to befall the Church. And yet Christians were now free to proclaim the Gospel openly to the whole world.

The Expansion
of Christianity

21

Though the end of the persecutions brought about the free and rapid expansion of Christianity, the Church's expansion did not take place without growing pains. From the Resurrection on, Christians tried to express in words the significance of Jesus. All Christians shared the feeling that in Jesus God was saying something to man. But as they tried to probe into the mystery of God's purpose and the person of Christ they ran into verbal and philosophical difficulties.

The First Council of Nicaea

In 313 the Church was particularly troubled by a controversy centering on two men: Arius and Athanasius. Arius, a priest of high intelligence and noble character from Alexandria, Egypt, spoke of Christ as God's first creation. Though Christ existed before time, "there was when he was not." And so, though Christ was better and more perfect than other men, and though he was created before them, Christ was nonetheless *part of creation* (and therefore not God, who is creator). In Arius' view, then, Christ was more than man (and therefore not really a human example to follow) and less than God (not really God entering human life). Christ was neither human nor divine.

Athanasius, a deacon from Alexandria, opposed the popular Arius and asserted that Christ was God flowing out of God into a human being. It was God himself who became a man in Jesus Christ. In effect, Athanasius was saying that

Christ was fully divine (in him we see what God is like)
and fully human (he shared all our temptations and agonies
and still showed what humanity could be at its richest and
best).

The dispute tore the Church into factions. Finally Church
leaders urged Constantine to summon a council of the world's
bishops to deal with the problem. Constantine, of course,
wanted to use Christianity to unite his empire and was
therefore concerned that Christianity itself not be divided.
He therefore summoned all the world's bishops to the town
of Nicaea (near Constantinople) in 325 to a general council
following the pattern of the Jerusalem Council (see chapter
19). Of the more than 300 bishops present, many bore visible
scars from the days of persecutions. Though the unbaptized
Constantine presided at the council, decisions were not
handed down by the emperor or by one particular bishop
claiming superiority over others. The bishops met, discussed
and argued, and decided by majority vote.

The main debate raged around the smallest letter in the
Greek alphabet, the iota (which is like our "i"). Arius and
his supporters insisted that Christ was *"like"* or *"similar to"*
the Father (in Greek, *homoiousion*). Athanasius and his
followers insisted that Christ was "of one substance with the
Father" (*homoousion,* in Greek). Opponents of Christianity
said Christians had little better to do than argue over an iota.

After lengthy debate all but two bishops took the view of
Athanasius and declared Arius' view heretical (wrong). They
then issued a creed (a statement of belief, from the Latin
credo, "I believe"). Simple creeds had been used very early
by converts professing belief before they were baptized.
Perhaps the earliest creed is found in Paul's letter to the Corinthian Church: "Jesus Christ is the Lord." Longer summaries
of the faith were in use by A.D. 100, as Christians added
phrases to combat what they considered to be faulty under-
standings of Jesus. Such was the case at Nicaea. The creed

that was issued makes only a very simple statement about God as Father and as Spirit, because those two aspects of God's activity were not disputed. But great care was spent in explaining Christ. Italicized words and phrases are those specially included to combat the Arian heresy.

We believe in one God the Father All-Sovereign, maker of all things visible and invisible.

And in one Lord Jesus Christ, the *Son* of God, begotten of the Father, only-begotten, that is, of *one substance of the Father,* God out of God, Light out of Light, *true God out of true God, begotten not made, of one substance with the Father, through whom all things were made, things in heaven and things on earth;* who for us men and for our salvation came down and was made flesh, and *became man,* suffered, and rose on the third day, ascended into the heavens, is coming to judge living and dead.

And in the Holy Spirit.

And those that say 'there was when he was not,' and, 'Before he was begotten he was not,' and that, 'He came into being from what-is-not,' or those that allege that the Son of God is 'of another substance or essence' or 'created,' or 'changeable' or 'alterable,' these the Catholic and Apostolic Church anathematizes.

The Church's beliefs were defined only after years of discussion and groping. In 381 the Council of Constantinople elaborated on parts of the Creed of Nicaea, and what we call the Nicene Creed (PB, 71) is this later elaboration. The Council of Chalcedon (451) attempted to deal with the difficulty of defining who Christ is. In the end it concluded that it was impossible to explain Christ, and, therefore, simply asserted the mystery of Christ: that he was both fully divine and fully human. In Christ God comes into his creation to show men his purpose for their lives. In the human life of Jesus we see what God is like and what man can be. Christ, as man, understands us; as God, he saves us:

Therefore, following the holy Fathers, we all with one accord teach men to acknowledge one and the same Son, our Lord Jesus Christ, at once complete in Godhead and complete in manhood, truly God and truly man; of one substance with the Father as regards his Godhead, at the same time of one substance with us as regards his manhood.

Monasticism

The decline and fall of the Roman Empire was underway before the Council of Nicaea. In the years after the council the empire steadily weakened. Inflation and decadence caused the government to rot from within, while the barbarians from the outside plundered first the imperial outposts and finally Rome itself in 410. In the centuries of chaos which followed, the monastic movement played the principal role in preserving European culture and learning. "Monasticism" comes from the Greek word for "alone." Monasticism arose in the East; the first monks were hermits who isolated themselves from the competitions and temptations of the world. As it moved west, monasticism grew less individualistic. By the fifth century western monasteries attracted hundreds of men and women and became strongholds of learning and social concern.

Like any group of people living together, monks and nuns had to have regulations. Benedict of Nursia (480-550) founded a vast monastery at Monte Cassino, and his regulations for it were so effective that they came to be adopted by most monastic communities in the West. The "Rule of St. Benedict" was threefold: poverty, chastity, and obedience. Monks were to have no property of their own, they were to remain unmarried so as to be able to devote their full energies to the service of God and man, and they were to submit their wills obediently to the abbot (or head monk) who was democratically elected by all.

So we are going to establish a school for the service of the Lord. In founding it we hope to introduce nothing harsh and burdensome, but if a certain strictness should result do not be dismayed and fly from the way of salvation, for its entrance cannot but be narrow.

The evil danger of owning private property should be entirely eradicated from the monastery. No one shall possess anything of his own, books, paper, pens, or anything else; for monks are not to own even their own bodies and wills to be used at their own desire, but are to look to the abbot of the monastery for everything. All things are to be had in common according to the command of the Scriptures.

[The monk is] not to yield to the desire of the flesh, not to wish to be called holy before he is so, but rather to strive to be holy so that he may be truly so called; [he is] to obey the commandments of God in his daily life, to love chastity.

Let everyone in the monastery obey the rule in all things, and let no one depart from it to follow the desires of his own heart. Let no one of the brethren presume to dispute the authority of the abbot, either within or outside the monastery. But the abbot should do all things in the fear of the Lord, knowing that he must surely render account to God, the righteous judge, for all his decisions.   Rule of St. Benedict

Benedict divided the day into periods of work (such as study, manual labor, farming, preaching, teaching, or nursing) and corporate worship. There were seven services of worship at regular intervals through the day.

The prophet says: "Seven times a day do I praise thee"; and we observe this sacred number of the seven services of the day; that is, lauds, prime, terce, sext, none, vespers, and compline.

These services served as reminders, in the midst of the day's work, that everything a monk did was to be done as an offering to God. "To pray is to work," wrote Benedict, "and to work is to pray." We can worship God truly only with our whole lives. Work not offered to God is selfish; prayer offered to God without the willingness to give our lives to him is hyprocritical.

Monasteries were self-sufficient. They grew their own food and made their own clothes. In the Dark Ages after the fall of the Roman Empire monasteries erected massive fortress defenses for protection. And in the political chaos of the following centuries they almost single-handedly preserved learning and culture. Practically no education took place in the Middle Ages outside the monasteries. And the only hospitals were those staffed by monks.

In the later Middle Ages, with the development of towns, a large population of helpless and poor emerged. To meet the needs of these poor, two orders sprang up, both founded by wealthy young men. Dominic (1170-1221) founded a preaching and teaching order, later called the Dominicans. And Francis of Assisi (1181-1226) founded an order of "little friars," not just to preach, but to work (preach by action) and live among the poor.

The Crusades

Europe had just begun to recover from the barbarian hordes when it was threatened, in the seventh century, by the rise of Islam. This religion, based on the teaching of Mohammed (570-629), grew rapidly in Palestine, Egypt, and North Africa and made inroads into a Europe weakened by barbarians and divided by feuding nobles. In 1071 the Mohammedan Seljuk Turks came into power in the Holy Land. Though Mohammed himself had pledged to respect the worship of Christians and Jews, the Turks desecrated the Christian holy places and mistreated Christian pilgrims who came to them.

In 1095, at the Council of Clermont, Pope Urban II issued

the call for a holy war—crusade—to rescue the holy places from the infidels. He hoped that, along with regaining the holy places, this common cause would unify the nobles and knights of Europe who were constantly engaged in fighting each other in petty wars. Here is what he said to them:

An accursed race has invaded the lands of the East. Christians are enslaved, tortured, killed. The swordsmen practice on them to see whether a neck can be cut in two with one blow. Churches are used as stables, or wrecked or turned into Mohammedan mosques. Who can take vengeance if not you who have won glory in arms? But you are swollen with pride and cut each other to pieces. Come now to the defense of Christ. Forget feuds; fight infidels. Before you is the standard bearer, leading you to war, the unseen standard bearer, even Christ.

Even though the pope had some good ends in mind (the end of European wars and the recovery of the holy places), his message, with its spirit of vengeance, is not one of history's most noble Christian documents. However, it provoked an immediate response. Most of Europe's nobility, as well as hundreds of thousands of peasants, were roused to action and set off for the Holy Land. Whatever religious fervor there was to begin with was soon mixed with more worldly motives. In 1099 the crusaders celebrated the capture of Jerusalem first by having a penitential procession of thanksgiving to Christ's tomb and then by slaughtering most of the town's inhabitants. As crusade succeeded crusade, material plunder became the main goal of most crusaders. After a brief time the holy places fell back into Mohammedan hands, and by 1291 not a Christian was left in the Holy Land.

The Papacy

By the sixth century, the bishops of five cities—Jerusalem, Antioch, Rome, Constantinople, and Alexandria—had come

to be regarded as head bishops in their areas and were known
as patriarchs or popes. Their task was to lead the Church in
their areas, to call meetings of the bishops under them when
necessary, and to secure aid for poorer bishops. The only
patriarch in Europe was the Bishop of Rome and he became
known in the Western Church as "*the* pope." In the East,
Mohammedan invasions overran all the churches except the
one in Constantinople, whose bishop was thus the only "free"
pope in the Eastern Church.

The Western pope called himself the success of Peter,
Rome's first bishop, and his claim to be "first among equals"
among his fellow bishops was accepted throughout the
Western Church. As early as 396, for example, St. Augustine
wrote of the Bishop of Rome: "Rome has spoken, the matter
is settled."

Such was not the case, however, in the East. For years the
Eastern and Western Churches had grown apart. There was
a language barrier (the East spoke Greek, the West, Latin).
Differences in liturgy, fasting, and doctrine were magnified
by the difficulties of communication. But the most crucial
argument concerned the Bishop of Rome's claim to supremacy over the whole Church, East and West. In 1054, when
the Patriarch of Constantinople refused to acknowledge the
Bishop of Rome's authority in the East, the Bishop of Rome
excommunicated him, upon which the patriarch excommunicated the pope. These mutual excommunications were not
revoked until this century.

In the West, however, the popes continued to advance
their supremacy not only in the Church but in the world.
With the fall of the Western Roman Empire, the pope
became the main political power in Italy. In the eighth century Charlemagne, chief of the Franks, conquered most of
what had been the Roman Empire. On Christmas Day 800,
Pope Leo III, without warning, in a brilliant maneuver suddenly crowned Charlemagne Roman Emperor. Charlemagne

was careful to exclude the pope from his son's coronation, but henceforth the popes would take Leo's crowning of Charlemagne as a precedent for the pope's right to choose and crown emperors.

Charlemagne's empire faded, and the late Middle Ages witnessed the emergence of the pope as the most powerful figure of the Western world. His word was absolute in the Church and he dominated the political scene. In 1077 Pope Gregory VII (Hildebrand) forced the world's most powerful king, Henry IV of Germany, to wait three days in the snow at Canossa, dressed as a penitent, for going against his wishes. He thus successfully rebuked Henry's attempt to appoint bishops to dioceses in Germany. Innocent III (1198-1216) proclaimed that he, the pope, "stands in the midst between God and man, below God, above man; less than God, more than man. He judges all, is judged by none." Gregory also claimed that Christ had left to Peter and his successor "not only the Church but the whole world." But Boniface VIII (1294-1303) put the papal claim most extremely: "We declare, announce, and define that it is altogether necessary for salvation for every human creature to be subject to the Roman pontiff."

This was the swan song of the medieval papacy, however. As Europe emerged from the Middle Ages, kings gained power and resisted papal control. King Philip IV of France secured the election of a Frenchman as pope in 1309, and until 1377 the kings of France exerted effective control over the popes who lived not in Rome but in Avignon, France. This is known as the Babylonian Captivity of the papacy, after the captivity of the Jews by the Babylonians, 604-562 B.C. From 1378 to 1417, though the popes returned to Rome, there was immense confusion about who was pope. The various claimants of the office kept excommunicating one another.

But the maneuvers of the popes are not the main story of

the Church in the Middle Ages. The period from the twelfth to the fourteenth century has been called the Age of Faith. Nowhere was this faith more dramatically demonstrated than in the building of the great cathedrals of Europe. The faith and genius of artists and builders combined with the devotion and sacrifice of nobles and peasants in what was perhaps the greatest flowering of creativity in human history.

Still, as the thirteenth century came to a close the Church everywhere showed signs of decadence and corruption. Its hierarchy grew rich and self-indulgent, popular religion was superstitious, the services of the Church were not understood, nor was the Bible read. As Europe emerged from the Middle Ages, sensitive and intelligent men everywhere cried for reform of the Church.

The Reformation   22

In the twelfth century, with the flowering of Gothic architecture and the increase in learning, European civilization had begun to come alive again. This rebirth culminated in the period known as the Renaissance (1350-1600). The feudalism of the Middle Ages (the thousands of local feudal lords throughout Europe, each with his castle, his lands, and his peasants) gave way to nationalism. Kings exerted control over the nobles. Emerging from the peasant class, a middle class of merchants and bankers began to establish itself in new towns. Copernicus revolutionized scientific thinking. Geniuses such as Michelangelo and Leonardo da Vinci ushered in a new era in sculpture and art. Explorers unveiled a whole New World. Everywhere society seemed injected with exuberance, creativity, and innovation.

The Church, however, failed to change with the times. There was little intellectual vitality, superstitions abounded, the Latin was not understood by the people, the Bible was untranslated and unread. The Church was corrupt. Simony (the sale of Church offices to the highest bidder) and nepotism (appointment of relatives to Church positions) were more the rule than the exception. The powerful Italian Medici family, for example, made one of its members, the future Pope Leo, a cardinal at fourteen. Some men were bishops of three or four dioceses at the same time and collected revenues from all of them without ever visiting them. And, worst of all, the household of the Church's leader, the pope, was the most corrupt and decadent court in Europe. Immense taxes were levied to maintain the papal court's elegance. One pope, Alexander VI, purchased the papacy by bribery, openly promoted the interests of his illegitimate children, and was probably a murderer.

The Protestant Revolution

Voices of protest about the Church's condition were heard everywhere in Europe. They found a single powerful expression in Martin Luther (1483-1546).

Martin Luther was a child of his time. His father, a peasant miner, had made his way as a merchant into the emerging middle class. Luther's family and education were religious in the conventional way. However, his upbringing seems to have been more than conventionally harsh and rigid. His father beat him bloody for trivial offenses, and he was often beaten at school, though he was a brilliant student. He enjoyed singing and had many friends, but there was about him a seriousness and intensity which set him apart from his fellow students.

His father's great ambition was that Martin go into law, a highly respected middle-class occupation. Luther, after finishing at the university in 1505, began training as a lawyer. In July 1505 his legal studies were abruptly halted.

Then Luther began telling the story of how when travelling not far from Erfurt he had been so shaken by a flash of lightning, that he cried out in terror, 'Help me St. Anne, and I will become a monk. Afterwards I regretted the vow and others tried to dissuade me. But I stuck to it. My father was angry about the vow, but I stuck to my decision. I never dreamed of leaving the monastery. I had quite died to the world.'

RUPP and DREWERY, A-4 (abridged)

After an initial period of happiness as a monk Luther seems to have been overwhelmed by a sense of his unworthiness. He turned to the medieval practices of self-punishment, rigid fasting, and endless prayer. All these only tended to

increase his guilt and despair over each failure to follow
Christ perfectly.

Between 1507 and 1519, however, Luther was able to resolve his personal crisis. He was now lecturer at the new
University of Wittenberg. In the course of lecturing on St.
Paul, he was suddenly struck by a phrase from Paul's Letter
to the Romans (1:17): "The just man finds life through
faith." The Pauline doctrine of "justification by faith" (see
chapter 19) became the guiding principle of his life and
eventually, through him, the battle cry of the Reformation.

Luther had previously thought of Christ as Judge. Now he
began to see him as the expression of God's love, God's reaching out to man. Paul had written (Ephesians 2:8): "It is by
his [God's] grace you are saved, through trusting him [faith];
it is not your own doing. It is God's gift, not a reward for
work done." God's grace (his gift of love in Christ) is freely
given. It cannot be earned by following prescribed laws or
even by doing good works. God's grace is received by faith
alone, by man's wholehearted response to and acceptance of
God's love. Luther did not discount good works. He saw
them as the fruits of man's faithful response to God's love,
rather than as the means of earning God's love.

As Luther attained positions of higher responsibility in the
Church (professor at Wittenberg, then head of eleven of his
order's monasteries) he became increasingly aware of the
Church's corruption. In 1510 he journeyed to Rome and saw
firsthand the decadence and wealth of the papal court. He
was horrified at the extravagant sums extorted from the poor
there on holy pilgrimages.

But the issue which finally roused Luther to public protest
was the sale of indulgences in Germany by Johann Tetzel, a
Dominican monk, agent of Pope Leo X. Leo is reputed to
have referred to the Gospel as a "fable" and, on becoming
pope in 1513, declared: "Now that God has given us the

papacy, let us enjoy it!" Because Leo's greatest enjoyment
was architecture, he sought to raise a vast sum of money to
build the largest and most richly decorated church on earth:
St. Peter's Basilica in Rome. Leo declared that those who
contributed to the building of St. Peter's would receive indulgences in proportion to the size of their contribution. The
selling of indulgences was a medieval practice: the theory
was that the saints (by their virtuous lives) had stored up a
"treasury of merits," and that payment of money to the
Church could purchase some of these merits to reduce one's
own sentence in purgatory, or to reduce the sentence of a
relative. Purgatory was the place to which the faithful went
after death to be purged from their sins.

Tetzel popularized Leo's indulgences by means of a catch
phrase: "As soon as money in the coffers rings, the soul from
purgatory's fire springs." Here is how a contemporary described Tetzel's appeal:

He gained by his preaching in Germany an immense sum of
money, all of which he sent to Rome; and especially at the
new mining works at St. Annaberg, where I, Frederick Mecum,
heard him for two years, a large sum was collected. It is incredible what this ignorant and impudent friar gave out. He
said that if a Christian [committed the worst possible crime]
and placed the sum of money in the Pope's indulgence chest,
the Pope had power in heaven and earth to forgive the sin,
and if he forgave it, God must do so also. Item, if they contributed readily and bought grace and indulgence, all the hills
of St. Annaberg would become pure massive silver. Item, so
soon as the coin rang in the chest, the soul for whom the
money was paid, would go straightway to heaven. The indulgence was so highly prized, that when the commissary entered
a city, the [Pope's decree on indulgences] was borne on satin
or gold, embroidered cushion, and all the priests and monks,
the town council, schoolmaster, scholars, men, women, maid-
ens, and children, went out to meet him with banners and

tapers, with songs and procession. Then all the bells were rung, all the organs played; he was conducted into the church, a red cross was erected in the midst of the church, and the Pope's banner displayed; in short, God himself could not have been welcomed and entertained with greater honour.

F. MYCONIUS, *Hist Ref. in* B. J. KIDD, *D.C.R.,* #9

Enraged, Luther wrote out 95 theses (propositions) in Latin and nailed them to the castle church's door at Wittenberg on October 31, 1517. Posting statements was the normal practice by which intellectual debates were carried on; there was therefore nothing unusual about Luther's action. Luther had no intention of breaking with the pope or the Church; in fact he was confident that if the pope found out about Tetzel's excesses he, too, would condemn him. Here are some of Luther's Theses.

21. Hence those preachers of Indulgences are wrong when say that a man is absolved and saved from every penalty by the Pope's Indulgences.

24. It must therefore follow that the greater part of the people are deceived by that indiscriminate and liberal-sounding promise of freedom from penalty.

27. It is mere human talk that the soul flies out [of purgatory] immediately the money clinks in the collection-box.

35. It is not Christian preaching to teach that those who aim to redeem their souls, or to purchase confessional Indulgences, have no need of contrition.

36. Any Christian whatsoever who is truly repentant has as his due, plenary remission from penalty and guilt, even without letters of Indulgence.

37. Any true Christian whatsoever, living or dead, participates in all benefits of Christ and the Church; and this is granted him by God, even without letters of Indulgence.

39. It is very difficult, even for the most learned theologians, to extol to the people at the same time the bounty of Indulgences and the need for true contrition.

40. True contrition seeks out and loves to pay the penalties of sin; whereas the bounty of Indulgences relaxes the penalties and makes men resent them—or at least it *can* do.

45. Christians should be taught that he who sees a needy person and passes him by, although he gives money for pardons, wins for himself not Papal Indulgences but the wrath of God.

50. Christians should be taught that, if the Pope knew the exactions of the preachers of Indulgences, he would rather have the basilica of St. Peter reduced to ashes than built with the skin, flesh and bones of his sheep.

67. The Indulgences, which the merchants extol as the greatest gifts of grace, are rightly understood as 'greatest' only as far as money-getting is concerned.

86. Again: 'Since the Pope's wealth is larger than that of the [richest millionaire] of our time, why does he not build this one basilica of St. Peter with his own money, rather than with that of the faithful poor?'   RUPP and DREWERY, D-5

In 1520 Luther publicly denied that either the pope or the councils of the Church were infallible in their decisions. He called for the princes to take Church reform into their own hands, a request which in some cases led princes to become local lay popes. There were not seven sacraments, he claimed, but only three: Baptism, Communion, and Penance. He insisted the wine be given to the people at Mass, rather than the bread alone.

The pope had felt at first that the theses were just part of an academic debate between two monastic orders, Luther's Augustinians and Tetzel's Dominicans. But by 1520 he saw the extent of Luther's desires for reform, condemned his writings as heretical, and ordered him to recant or be excommunicated. Luther contemptuously burnt the pope's decree in public and was excommunicated.

The civil authority, the Diet (or parliament) of the Holy

Roman Emperor, meeting at Worms in 1521, ordered Luther to recant. To this Luther responded:

Since your serene Majesty and your Lordships request a simple answer, I shall give it, with no strings and no catches. Unless I am convinced by the testimony of scripture or plain reason (for I believe neither in Pope nor councils alone, since it is agreed that they have often erred and contradicted themselves), I am bound by the scriptures I have quoted, and my conscience is captive to the Word of God. I neither can nor will revoke anything, for it is neither safe nor honest to act against one's own conscience.   RUPP and DREWERY, I-1

Luther was banned from the empire and his life was threatened. But the Elector of Saxony, a prince of the empire, became his protector. Revolution broke out everywhere in the Church: monks and nuns left their monasteries, priests married, images and shrines were destroyed. Luther himself married a nun in 1525.

While Luther had not intended to break away from the Church, by 1530 he and his followers had effectively formed their own church. As time went on, Luther allowed the ordaining of priests without bishops, translated the liturgy into German, gave the people both the bread and the wine at the Lord's Supper, denied purgatory, condemned celibacy and monasticism, and repudiated the pope's authority. One of Luther's great achievements was his composing of hymns to encourage participation by the people in public worship. Hymns such as "A Mighty Fortress is Our God" have remained popular for 450 years. His translation of the Bible into German put the Bible into the hands of the people for the first time and greatly influenced the development of the German language.

By his death in 1546, Lutheranism had established itself in many parts of Germany. Finally in 1555 the Peace of

Augsburg established the right of princes throughout the empire to decide whether Christianity in their area would be Roman Catholic or Lutheran. But Luther had opened a Pandora's box. Within fifty years hundreds of small Christian splinter groups arose, each with its own distinctive customs and beliefs. Luther's own reforms had been quite conservative. Others soon went beyond him.

Ulrich Zwingli (1484-1531), without being influenced by Luther, advanced many of the same reforms in Zurich. He had all relics, pictures, statues, and organs removed from churches, and he confiscated monastic properties. He understood the Lord's Supper as merely symbolic. Christ, he said, was not present in the Lord's Supper, but only remembered. The Catholic Church, and even Luther, claimed that a church custom could be practiced if it did not violate Scripture. Zwingli, however, was a radical biblicist, and insisted that a custom must be abolished unless a specific precedent could be found for it in the Bible. This Bible-centeredness became characteristic of a large number of Protestant sects throughout Europe and eventually America.

The most prominent Reformation figure besides Luther was John Calvin (1509-1564). He had none of Luther's flair or personal appeal. By birth and background a French aristocrat, he was dry, simple, and austere in his personal life. Driven from Paris in 1533 because of his reform views, he was prevailed upon in 1536 to accept the post of pastor at Geneva. Here, after controversy and a brief exile, he established a "theocratic" state. He insisted that every citizen of Geneva had to make formal profession of his (Calvin's) statement of faith or be exiled from the city. He instituted a complex, democratically elected government which combined church and state and laid down laws which enforced a strict and somber code of morality. Frivolities such as dancing, games, and colored clothes were forbidden. The descendants of Calvin are called "Presbyterians," since the assembly of elders (presbyters) was the principal governing unit in Calvin's organizational scheme.

It is difficult to evaluate the Reformation as a whole. No one can deny the crying need for reform that existed in the Church when Luther posted his theses. But it is a mistake to think of the results of the Reformation as entirely good. The unity of the Church was shattered. For centuries Europe was bloodied by religious wars between Catholics and Protestants. The local Protestant churches, free from the corrupting influence of the papacy, frequently fell under the influence of local political powers whose effect was at least as corrupt as the pope's had been.

The Catholic Reformation

In 1534 Paul III became pope. Though a typical Renaissance pope in his personal life (expensive tastes and four children), in his official life he encouraged reform of the Church. He appointed commissions, helped establish new monastic orders, surrounded himself with able theologians, but, most important of all, he called the great Council of Trent which met from 1545-1563. This Council redefined and reaffirmed the Catholic faith and asserted the pope's supreme authority in the Church. The Council and popes recognized and empowered several of the new religious orders which had suddenly and astonishingly sprung up. Most famous of these was the Society of Jesus (Jesuits) founded by Ignatius of Loyola (1491-1556). Members of this order placed themselves entirely in the hands of the pope, to do as he requested. Soon they began everywhere in Europe to open schools, seminaries, and colleges to teach the faith. By the end of the sixteenth century the papal court was a model of morality; intelligent preaching and teaching had removed many of the superstitious practices of the Middle Ages. The Catholic Church had been rejuvenated.

The Church
in England

23

We do not know how Christianity first came to England. Legend says that Joseph of Arimathaea (in whose tomb Jesus was buried) fled after the burial with twelve companions to England, taking with him the Holy Grail, the cup that had been used at the Last Supper. Another legend says that Joseph was a tinsmith who was engaged in regular trade between west England and Phoenicia (near Palestine), and that he brought the boy Jesus with him on one of his trips. At Glastonbury, where Joseph is alleged to have come with his companions, an oriental thorn, unknown elsewhere in England, blossoms twice each year: in May and on Christmas Day. The plant is supposed to have grown up in the spot where Joseph placed his staff on the ground upon arrival.

More probably, however, Christianity came to England with the Roman troops and traders who were present there for 450 years after Julius Caesar's invasion of Britain in 55 B.C. About A.D. 305 we have the first recorded martyrdom in Britain: a Roman Soldier, Alban, was beheaded for sheltering a priest who had converted and baptized him. We know that three British bishops were present at the Council of Arles in 314. Clearly, therefore, Christians in England were recognized as a true branch of the Church.

But in 409, as the Roman Empire crumbled, the Romans withdrew from Britain. In 449 Jutes, Angles, and Saxons invaded Britain. These Germanic invaders stamped out Christianity in England; only a few Christians were able to flee to the far west of England and to Wales where they huddled together in isolation.

The Celtic Church

In 405 a sixteen-year-old boy named Patrick was captured in England by a raiding party and taken to Ireland as a slave. After much suffering, he escaped Ireland by ship and went to France where he entered a monastery. Here he became certain that God wanted him to return to Ireland to strengthen Christianity there, and finally in 432 his superiors made him bishop of the Irish. His success in Ireland was immediate. What had been a group of scattered Christian communities became united. At Patrick's death in 461, Christianity was firmly established everywhere in Ireland.

Because Europe was in political chaos after Rome's fall, and because an island of pagans (Britain) separated Ireland from Europe, the Irish (called Celtic) Church was isolated from the mainstream of western Christianity. Its customs and outlook therefore developed independently of European influence. The Celtic Church adopted a different way of arriving at the date of Easter. Dioceses (groups of churches under a bishop's care) were based not on geography, but on existing tribes. The monastic communities were the heart of the Celtic Church, and in the next three centuries they were to become the center of western intellectual life and a refuge for European scholars.

But the most distinctive feature of Celtic Christianity was its passionate mystic fervor combined with extreme self-denial. In 563 the Celtic monk Columba (521-597) established, with his fellow monks, a base on the Island of Iona off the west coast of Scotland. From here they hoped to convert Britain to Christianity. Columba is described as having used bare rock as a mattress, and a stone for a pillow. In 635 Aidan, one of the Celtic monks on Iona, finally undertook the long-anticipated project of converting Britain. The obvious sanctity of this fervent Celt's life drew vast numbers in northern England and Scotland to the faith. The historian Bede writes:

Whether in town or country, he always travelled on foot unless compelled by necessity to ride; and whatever people he met on walks, whether high or low, he stopped and spoke to them. All who walked with him, whether monks or layfolk, were required to meditate. If, on rare occasions, he was invited to dine with the king, when he had eaten sparingly, he left as soon as possible to read or pray. Many were inspired to follow his example and adopted the practice of fasting. If wealthy people did wrong, he never kept silent out of fear or respect, but corrected them outspokenly. If the wealthy ever gave him gifts of money, he either distributed it for the needs of the poor or used it to ransom any who had been unjustly sold as slaves.   E.H. 3:5 (abridged)

The Roman Mission

About 585, shortly before he became pope, Pope Gregory I was standing in the market place in Rome. Bede describes what happened.

Some merchants who had recently arrived in Rome displayed their many wares in the market-place. Among the crowd who thronged to buy was Gregory, who saw among other merchandise some boys exposed for sale. These had fair complexions, fine-cut features, and beautiful hair. Looking at them with interest he enquired from what country and what part of the world they came. 'They come from the island of Britain,' he was told, 'where all the people have this appearance.' He then asked whether the islanders were Christians, or whether they were still ignorant heathens. 'They are pagans,' he was informed. 'Alas!' said Gregory with a heartfelt sigh: 'how sad that such bright-faced folk are still in the grasp of the Author of darkness, and that such graceful features conceal minds void of God's grace! What is the name of this race?' 'They are called Angles', he was told. 'That is appropriate,' he said, 'for they have angelic faces, and it is right that they should become joint-heirs with the angels in heaven. And what is the name of the Province from which they have been brought?' 'Deira', was the answer. 'Good. They shall indeed be rescued *de ira*—from wrath—and called to the mercy of Christ. And what is the name of their king?' 'Aelle', he was told. 'Then,' said Gregory, making a play on the name, 'it is right that their land should echo the praise of God our Creator in the word *Alleluia*.'

E.H. 2:1

When Gregory became Pope he decided to send one of his monks, Augustine, to convert the Angles. Augustine was afraid and reluctant to go to faraway England, but obediently set out with a band of forty monks.

Having undertaken this task in obedience to the pope's command and progressed a short distance on their journey, they become afraid. For they were appalled at the idea of going to a barbarous, fierce, and pagan nation, of whose very language they were ignorant. They unanimously agreed that to turn back was the safest course and sent back Augustine so that he might humbly request the holy Gregory to recall them from so dangerous, arduous, and uncertain a journey. In reply the Pope wrote, 'Gregory, Servant of the servants of God, to the servants of our Lord. My very dear sons, it is better never to undertake any high enterprise than to abandon it once begun. So with the help of God you must carry out this holy task which you have begun.'

E.H. 1:23 (abridged)

Arriving in Canterbury they were greeted by the king whose first words were "Stop right where you are." After he had talked with them, however, he was impressed by their courage and sincerity.

'Your words and promises are fair indeed; but they are new
and uncertain, and I cannot accept them and abandon the
age-old beliefs that I have held, together with the whole English nation. But since you have travelled far, and I see that
you are sincere in your desire to impart to us what you believe
to be true and excellent, we will not harm you. Nor will we
forbid you to preach and win any people you can to your
religion.'   *E.H.* 1:25 (abridged)

The monks proceeded to Canterbury. Though people were
not much impressed by their speaking, they gradually were
drawn to Christianity as they observed the quality of life the
monks lived.

They practiced what they preached. Before long a number of
heathen, admiring the simplicity of their holy lives and the
comfort of their heavenly message, believed and were baptised.
At length the king himself, among others, edified by the pure
lives of these holy men and their gladdening promises, believed
and was baptised.   *E.H.* 1:26 (abridged)

Within a few months over 10,000 had become baptized
Christians.

In 601, to reinforce Augustine's growing mission in the
south, Pope Gregory sent another mission to Northumbria in
the north of England. The leader was Paulinus, who at once
set to work converting the king of the area. The king,
Edwin, was married to a Christian but still clung to the old
pagan religion of his father. Bede describes the king's agonizing doubts about whether to become a Christian.

He used to sit alone for hours, as I have said, earnestly de-
liberating what he should do and what religion he should
follow. On one of the occasions, the man of God [Paulinus]
came to him: 'Hesitate no longer. Accept the Faith and keep
the commands of Him who has delivered you from all your
earthly troubles and raised you to the glory of an earthly king-

dom. If you will henceforth obey his will, he will save you likewise from the everlasting doom of the wicked and give you a
place in His eternal kingdom in heaven.' When he heard this,
the king answered that it was his will as well as his duty to
accept the Faith that Paulinus taught, but said that he must
discuss the matter with his principal advisers and friends, so
that, if they were in agreement, they might all be cleansed
together in Christ the Fount of Life.   *E.H.* 2:12-13

Calling together his council, he was given this advice by one
of the elders:

'Your Majesty, when we compare the present life of man
on earth with that time of which we have no knowledge, it
seems to me like the swift flight of a single sparrow through the
banqueting-hall where you are sitting at dinner on a winter's
day with your counsellors. In the midst there is a comforting
fire to warm the hall; outside, the storms of the winter rain or
snow are raging. This sparrow flies swiftly in through one door
of the hall, and out through another. While he is inside, he
is safe from the winter storms; but after a few moments of
comfort, he vanishes from sight into the wintry world from
which he came. Even so, man appears on earth for a little
while; but of what went on before this life or of what follows,
we know nothing. Therefore, if this new teaching has brought
any more certain knowledge, it seems only right that we should
follow it.'   *E.H.* 2:13 (abridged)

Upon receiving this advice the king and his whole council
were baptized.

The United Church of Britain

Inevitably the Celtic Church in the north under Aidan
spread to the south and met the Roman missions begun in
England by Augustine and Paulinus coming north. Each
group regarded the other with suspicion. The customs of the

long-isolated Celtic Church were regarded as perversions by the Roman mission, while the Roman Christians were regarded as foreign intruders by the Celts. However, they overcame their differences with remarkable speed.

Wilfrid (634-709), a monk who had studied under Aidan at Lindisfarne, the great Scottish Celtic monastery, made a pilgrimage to Rome in 653 and came back to persuade most of his fellow Celtic Christians to accept the Roman customs. In 664, both groups met at the Synod of Whitby and the Celts agreed to adopt Roman practices. In 668 the pope appointed Theodore of Tarsus to be archbishop of Canterbury. He had had no connection with the English Church or its controversies and was able skillfully to reconcile and unite all elements.

Within a hundred years of Theodore's landing, Britain was solidly Christian. In the eighth century and after, as Europe was immersed in chaos, the old Celtic monasteries became the centers in which civilization was preserved and scholarship and devotion encouraged. It was largely due to the efforts of English missionaries in this period that Christianity was kept alive in many parts of Europe.

The Conflict of Pope and King

Because Britain was an island, a strong sense of national identity developed earlier there than on the Continent. The years after the Norman Conquest of England in 1066 were marked by almost continual bickering between the popes and the English kings. When Pope Gregory VII tried to get King William the Conqueror to do him homage in 1075, William resisted: "I refuse to do fealty and I shall not do it; for I did not promise it nor do I find that my predecessors did fealty to yours."

The most famous clash between pope and king was between the pope's representative, Archbishop Thomas à

Becket, and King Henry II. Becket blocked the king's interference in Church affairs. Four noblemen regarded the king's
frustration with Becket as an indication that they should
murder Becket and, to the king's horror, they killed him in
Canterbury Cathedral in 1170. The Church almost instantly
declared Thomas a saint, and for centuries his shrine was the
most popular place of pilgrimage in Europe. Chaucer wrote
of the Canterbury pilgrims:

And specially from every shire's end
Of England to Canterbury they wend;
The holy, blissful martyr for to seek
That them hath holpen when that they were sick.

The popes levied heavy taxes on England, and in 1213 Pope
Innocent III forced King John to bow down to his representative and swear that he owed his right to reign to the
pope. However, two years later, in 1215, the English nobles,
led by Archbishop Stephen Langton, compelled John to sign
the Magna Carta which guaranteed that "the Church of England shall be free, and shall have her rights entire and her
liberties uninjured." Every English monarch since has been
obliged to reconfirm the Charter. By the time of King Edward III (1327-1377) the king and nobles were able to declare that neither the king nor any other person could
subject the nation to another power without the nation's
consent. Annual payments to the papal treasury ("Peter's
pence") were stopped for a time as well as annates (a bishop's first year's earnings which had to be paid entirely to the
pope). The next hundred years saw a continual battle between pope and king over these issues.

By the fourteenth century the English Church as a whole,
like the European Church, was sunk in superstition and corruption. Men were frequently appointed bishops of, and
collected vast sums from, dioceses which they never even
visited. Cardinal Wolsey (1475-1530), for example, was

bishop of three dioceses simultaneously and amassed a huge fortune. Indulgences were sold everywhere. The Bible was untranslated and unavailable to the people. Magical and superstitious teachings about the sacraments abounded. In winter, country parish churches often housed cattle six days a week.

Henry VIII and the Break with Rome

The long-needed reform of the Catholic Church in England came about as the result of the break of King Henry VIII with the pope. The English Reformation was essentially not a religious revolution but rather a political one. Henry VIII did not found a new church, as the European reformers had done. Under Henry, the Catholic Church in England freed itself from the pope's control and purged itself of certain corrupt practices.

Henry VIII was the ideal Renaissance prince; handsome, athletic, a learned scholar, an enthusiastic musical composer, he was highly popular. Early in his reign the pope awarded him the title "Defender of the Faith" for his writings in defense of the Catholic faith against Luther. Though Henry was irked by the constant interference of the pope in English affairs and by the pope's demand for money, Henry never in his life had any desire to change the faith and practice of the Church from what it was at the start of his reign.

Henry's father, Henry VII, tried to reunite Britain after the divisive War of the Roses. Of utmost importance was a stable ruling family, and Henry VII was determined to line up a strong successor to the throne. He therefore arranged the marriage of his eldest son Arthur to Catherine of Aragon (daughter of Ferdinand and Isabella of Spain). However, Arthur died at the age of 16, shortly after the marriage. Henry VII then promptly arranged for the marriage of his son Henry, then eleven years old, to Catherine. The proposed marriage was a specific violation not only of the Church's law, but of Scripture. Leviticus 20:21 reads: "If a man takes his brother's wife it is impurity; . . . they shall be childless" (RSV). For this reason two popes refused to allow the marriage, through a third finally gave his permission.

At age 17 Henry VIII became king and married Catherine who was 26. To secure the succession Henry wanted a son. Of the five children Catherine bore Henry, only one lived past infancy and that was a girl, Mary. By 1527 Catherine was well over 40, and the prospects of a male heir were poor. Henry regarded the mortality of their children as a sign of divine wrath at their illegal marriage. He therefore asked the pope not for a divorce, but for an annulment, since the marriage should never have taken place. That same year he fell in love with Anne Boleyn and desired to marry her and have a son by her.

Popes frequently granted annulments with far less reason: Louis VII and Eleanor his queen, who had many children of both sexes, were granted an annulment on the grounds of "incompatibility of mind." However, Henry's queen, Catherine, was the aunt of Charles V, King of Spain and Holy Roman Emperor. When Charles opposed the annulment, the pope was not strong enough to go against the wishes of Europe's most powerful king. He therefore stalled.

After four years of waiting, Henry grew impatient and pressured Parliament and the Convocation of the Church to end papal authority in England. The English bishops, gathering in 1531, declared that "the Bishop of Rome hath not by scripture any greater authority in England than any other foreign bishop," and that Henry was "Protector, simple and supreme Lord, and *so far as the Law of Christ allows*, even supreme head of the Church in England."

In 1532 Henry began living with Anne Boleyn. In January 1533 he secretly married her. In March, Thomas Cranmer, the Archbishop of Canterbury, nullified Henry's marriage to

Catherine. Anne was crowned queen in June. In July, the pope excommunicated Henry. And in September, Elizabeth was born to the newly-married couple. In 1534 parliament ratified Henry's supremacy over the English Church and again abolished Peter's pence and legal appeals to Rome. Supporters of the pope were exiled or put to death. Thus ended the thousand-year dominance of the English Church by the Bishop of Rome.

Henry's personal life grew steadily more degenerate. He became fat and alcoholic. He married no less than six wives before he died, and executed those, such as Thomas More, who criticized his marriages. He dissolved and looted many monasteries mainly for his own gain (though he did found several schools for the poor with part of the proceeds).

Yet while Henry was alive he allowed few changes of any importance in the principal beliefs and practices of the Church. He did, however, make a few reforms. Largely owing to his initiative, the Bible was translated for the first time into English. By the Royal Injunctions of 1538, Henry decreed that it be made available to the people:

You shall provide on this side the feast of Easter next coming, one book of the whole Bible of the largest volume, in English, and the same set up in some convenient place within the said church that you have cure of, whereat your parishioners may most commodiously resort to the same, and read it. And, that you shall discourage no man privately or publicly from the reading or hearing of the said Bible, but shall expressly provoke, stir, and exhort every person to read the same, as that which is the very lively word of God, that every Christian man is bound to embrace, believe, and follow, if he look to be saved; admonishing them nevertheless to avoid all contention and altercation herein, and to use an honest sobriety in the inquisition of the true sense of the same, and refer the explication of obscure places to men of higher judgment in Scripture.

Since the people were in total ignorance of even the fundamentals of Christianity, he decreed:

You shall every Sunday and holy day through the year openly and plainly recite to your parishioners twice or thrice together, or oftener, if need require, one particle or sentence of the 'Pater noster' ("Our Father") or Creed, in English, to the intent they may learn the same by heart, and so from day to day to give them one like lesson or sentence of the same till they have learned the whole "Pater noster" and Creed, in English, by rote; and as they be taught every sentence of the same by rote, you shall expound and declare the understanding of the same unto them, exhorting all parents and householders to do, and that done you shall declare unto them the Ten Commandments, one by one, every Sunday and holy day, till they be likewise perfect in the same.

Since superstition was common and because sermons and other teaching had long been omitted from church services, Henry further decreed:

You shall make, or cause to be made in the said church, and every other cure you have, one sermon every quarter of the year at the least, wherein you shall purely and sincerely declare the very gospel of Christ, and in the same exhort your hearers to the works of charity, mercy, and faith, specially prescribed and commanded in Scripture.

Turmoil and Settlement

Nine-year-old Edward VI succeeded his father, Henry VIII, as king. A regency of unscrupulous princes dominated his reign (1547-1553). They sought to reform the Church radically, in line with the Protestant reformers on the Continent. Not only did they try to seize control of the Church and change its faith and practices, but they looted the monasteries and desecrated churches for their own financial advantage and to enrich their homes.

By 1549, Thomas Cranmer, still archbishop of Canterbury had compiled the Book of Common Prayer, largely English translations of older Latin services. The bishops made it official. The continental Protestants, however, cried for a thorough rejection of Catholic faith and in 1552 pushed the English ruling princes to issue another Prayer Book which came close to denying the Catholic faith. The new book was issued without the bishops' permission.

This apostasy and wanton destruction was ended by the early death of Edward and the accession of Queen Mary. Under Mary, an ardent Roman Catholic like her mother Catherine, the pendulum swung the other way. Her principal aim was to restore England's subservience to the pope. Protestant princes and religious leaders were exiled and over 300 put to death. Though the bloodshed was probably no greater than that of the two previous reigns, the intolerant and emotional queen was unpopular and soon had earned the name "Bloody Mary." But Mary's reign was also short; she died in 1558.

After these two disastrous reigns, Elizabeth (1558-1603) became queen, established peace, and settled the English Church in a moderate position between Protestantism and Romanism. The Prayer Book of 1559 was a repudiation both of Protestant heresies and Roman abuses. Since the time of Elizabeth the character of the English Church, as both Catholic and reformed, has been broad and inclusive.

The Catholic Church of England had separated itself from control of the Bishop of Rome and had reformed itself from within. The apostolic faith remained in all its fullness, worship was purified of medieval superstitions, and the government of the Church by bishops in succession from the apostles was never broken. Archbishop Bramhall commented: "It is the same garden; we have simply pulled out the weeds."

The Coming
Great Church

24

Anglican or English Christianity was brought to the new world by English settlers. In 1579 the English explorer Sir Francis Drake landed briefly near San Francisco Bay, and his chaplain conducted a service there from the English Prayer Book while a small group of bewildered Indians looked on.

The American Episcopal Church

The real foundation of the English Church in America, however, took place in 1607, thirteen years before the pilgrims landed at Plymouth, when English settlers arrived in Virginia. The Rev. Robert Hunt, chaplain to the settlers, celebrated Holy Communion at Jamestown the day after landing. Captain John Smith described the scene.

We did hang an awning (which is an old sail) to three or four trees. . . . Till we cut planks, our pulpit was a bar of wood nailed to two neighboring trees. This was our church until we built a homely thing like a barne. . . . Yet we had daily Common Prayer morning and evening, every Sunday two sermons, and every three months Holy Communion.

Though the Church in Virginia was established by law as the official religion, as it expanded to other colonies it was, at best, only partially established as official. The Puritans fiercely resisted every attempt to establish Anglican churches in New England, and only after 1688 was the Church of England tolerated there.

The English Church in America fell under the jurisdiction of the bishop of London. Since the bishop never came to the colonies, and since parliament refused to assign a resident bishop to the colonies, the colonial Church was terribly handicapped. Without bishops there was no leadership, little unity, lax discipline, and no one to ordain or to confirm. Anyone wishing to be a priest had to pay for a trip to England to seek a bishop there who could ordain him. Nevertheless, the Church grew and prospered. Between 1701 and 1776 the Society for the Propagation of the Gospel sent over 350 missionaries from England to the colonies. The Church established William and Mary College in 1693 and in 1754 King's College, now Columbia. In 1722 the faculty of Yale abandoned Puritanism in favor of Anglicanism.

The American Revolution was a disaster for the English Church. Though George Washington and 35 of the 56 signers of the Declaration of Independence were Anglicans, many clergy and church members were loyal to the crown and when war broke out either returned to England or went to Canada. The expulsion of the British in 1783 meant the end of missionaries and money from the Society for the Preservation of the Gospel.

The time had come for the Church in America to be independent of the English Church. In 1783 the clergy of Connecticut elected Samuel Seabury as their bishop and sent him to England to be consecrated. Seabury had been a chaplain in the British army and, in 1775, had been briefly imprisoned for his loyalist views. The English bishops, however, were not legally allowed to consecrate Seabury, since he refused to take the required oath of loyalty to the king. Seabury then proceeded to Scotland where he was consecrated at Aberdeen on November 14, 1784, by three bishops of the Scottish Episcopal Church (the Church of England in Scotland). Parliament soon changed the loyalty oath requirement, and in 1787 two more Americans were made bishops, this time in England by English bishops. Church custom has always required three bishops to consecrate a new bishop in order to ensure the safety of the apostolic succession, so now that it possessed three of its own bishops, the American Church became self-sustaining.

In 1789 Church members from all the colonies met together in General Convention at Philadelphia. Many of the same men who devised the American Constitution were instrumental in setting up the constitution of the new Church. A two-house legislature, the first of bishops and the second of clergy and laity, was created. A Prayer Book similar to that of the English Church was adopted. The Preface to the new Prayer Book acknowledged the American Church's foundation by

The Church of England, to which the Protestant Episcopal Church in these States is indebted, under God, for her first foundation and a long continuance of nursing care and protection. . . . This Church is far from intending to depart from the Church of England in any essential point of doctrine, discipline, or worship; or further than local circumstances require.

The title "Protestant Episcopal Church in the United States of America" was chosen as the official name. The term "protestant" was not then, as it is now, associated with the European reformers such as Luther. It was used to show that though the Church had bishops and priests and sacraments, it was not a Roman (or papist) Church. Some say the word originates from the Latin words *pro* and *testo*, meaning "testify for," and that the Church's name indicates that this Church "testifies for" episcopacy (government by bishops). Since the word "protestant" is so misleading, it is rarely used in connection with the Episcopal Church today.

The Anglican Communion

The American Episcopal Church is one of twenty national and regional churches which are the historical children of the Church of England and which received their bishops from the English succession. These churches, with a combined membership of 46 million, are known collectively as the Anglican Communion.

The Anglican Communion is sometimes called "the bridge Church" because it stands between Protestantism and Roman Catholicism. Though Catholic in its government, worship, and belief, the Anglican Communion has freed itself from the dominance of the Bishop of Rome, the pope, and from the superstitions that crept into the Church in the Middle Ages. Anglicans are often called Catholics by Protestants and Protestants by Roman Catholics. Though we are Catholics, we are not Roman but rather *English* Catholics. Since we are not Roman, Roman Catholics label us Protestants. Though we are reformed, we still cannot properly be called Protestant as the reformation of the Church of England came from within and did not involve the founding of a new Church.

The Anglican Communion has been called "the broadest Church in Christendom" because it encompasses so vast an array of theological and liturgical viewpoints. One may, in the same town, attend an Anglican church offering a solemn high Mass and then go down the street to another Anglican church whose worship is simpler than any Protestant church in town. One Anglican bishop may question almost every clause of the Creed while another has dogmatically conservative views on moral and theological questions. The genius of Anglicanism has been to preserve unity and encourage diversity.

The leaders of the Anglican Communion came very early to recognize the key position of Anglicanism in the Ecumenical Movement. In 1888 the Lambeth Conference of Anglican bishops laid down four essential points of faith and order which they hoped to use for discussing with other churches the unity of all Christians. These points are called the Lambeth Quadrilateral.

1. The Holy Scriptures of the Old and New Testament, "containing all things necessary to salvation," are the ultimate rule and standard of faith.

2. The Apostles' Creed is the baptismal confession of belief; the Nicene Creed is the sufficient statement of the Christian faith.

3. The two sacraments ordained by Christ Himself—Baptism and the Supper of the Lord—ministered with unfailing use of Christ's words of institution and of the elements ordained by Him.

4. The historic episcopate, locally adapted in the methods of its administration to the varying needs of the nations and peoples called by God into the unity of his Church.

The Ecumenical Movement

For centuries efforts have been made to reunite the scattered Christian churches of the world. However, these efforts did not bear much fruit until this century. In 1910 the Edinburgh Missionary Conference gathered representatives from about 160 missionary societies of the Anglican and Protestant churches. This conference led to much greater cooperation by the churches in the mission field. Out of the Edinburgh experience grew a number of meetings in the next few decades which went into all the ramifications of what separated Christian bodies. In 1947 a great ecumenical step was taken in the creation of the Church of South India, in which Anglicans, Methodists, Presbyterians, Congregationalists, and Dutch Reformed Christians were united. And in 1948 the World Council of Churches was formed as "a fellowship of Churches which accept our Lord Jesus Christ as God and Saviour." The Council now has representatives from 150 Anglican, Orthodox, and Protestant religious groups, has brought about cooperation and understanding among denominations, and helped to coordinate the missionary efforts of the various churches. On the national scene the most promising effort at union of Episcopalians with various Protestant bodies is the present Consultation on Church Union (COCU), which may bring together nine American denominations.

But, of course, there can be no true Church unity without the world's largest body of Christians, the Roman Catholics. At the Catholic Reformation, the Council of Trent declared that the Roman Church was the true Church, and called upon all Christians to submit to the authority of the Bishop of Rome. In the eyes of non-Roman Christians the greatest block in the path to unity is the authority claimed for the pope by the Roman Church. In 1870 the First Vatican Council effectively relegated all authority in the Church to the pope, declaring that under certain conditions his views were infallible.

We (Pope Pius IX), adhering faithfully to the tradition received from the beginning of the Christian faith—with a view to the glory of our Divine Saviour, the exaltation of the Catholic religion, and the safety of Christian peoples (the Sacred Council approving), teach and define as a dogma divinely revealed: That the Roman Pontiff, when he speaks ex cathedra (that is, when—fulfilling the office of Pastor and Teacher of all Christians —on his supreme Apostolical authority, he defines a doctrine concerning faith or morals to be held by the Universal Church), through the divine assistance promised him in blessed Peter, is endowed with that infallibility, with which the Divine Redeemer has willed that His Church—in defining doctrine concerning faith or morals—should be equipped: And therefore, that such definitions of the Roman Pontiff of themselves—and not by virtue of the consent of the Church—are irreformable. If anyone shall presume (which God forbid!) to contradict this our definition, let him be anathema.

Vatican Council, Session IV. Cap. 4

The statement that "such definitions of the Roman Pontiff of themselves—*and not by virtue of the consent of the Church*—are irreformable" represents the furthest possible departure from the early Church's democratic conciliar form of government which was established at the Council of Jerusalem (chapter 19).

Another hindrance to union has been the tendency of the Roman Church to elevate the importance of Mary. In 1854 the Roman Church declared that Mary had been immaculately conceived. The dogma of the Immaculate Conception (which is not to be confused with the virgin birth of Jesus) declares that at the moment of Mary's conception a miracle occurred which freed her from the taint of original sin. And in 1950 the pope declared that at the moment of her death, "Mary was in body and soul assumed into heavenly glory." For neither of these doctrines, of course, is there a shred of scriptural or historical evidence, and non-Romans regard them as dangerous superstitions.

Many of the barriers of prejudice and suspicion between Romans and non-Romans were broken down singlehandedly by John XXIII who became pope in 1958. John's simplicity and warmth made him the hero of Protestants as well as Roman Catholics, and his joyful attitude swept away the frigid and rigid outlook that had characterized many of his predecessors. In 1962 he summoned the Second Vatican Council. It has enacted many of the reforms made years ago by non-Romans: for example, services in the language of the people and lay participation in the government of the Church. The council even took an important step away from concentrating all authority on the pope; it placed greater emphasis on the role of bishops as collective leaders of the Church. Representatives of all churches were invited to observe the council, and a new era of ecumenical dialogue was begun. The Roman Church today is engaged in unity discussions with virtually every major Christian body.

The Second Vatican Council revealed a very surprising variety of viewpoints within the Roman Church. Certainly Anglicans, Protestants, and Orthodox Christians have been aware of diversities among themselves for a long time. But what has begun to become apparent is that all major Christian bodies are fundamentally in agreement on major issues, and that customs (kneeling versus sitting, for example) are of minor importance. More and more Church leaders are coming to understand Church reunion in terms of "unity with diversity," in which all the richness of variation in customs of each of the various Christian bodies will be preserved.

The Church

The Church is often called "the Body of Christ." It is the company of Christ's followers and carries on all that Jesus tried to do in his lifetime. It is the extension of the Incarnation. In every age and place the Church proclaims the same Christ, though the terms of that proclamation, the words and actions in which it is couched, may vary.

As the extension of the Incarnation the Church is divine. Its calling is to be the means or instrument by which God's will is made known to men. And it has Christ's promise of ultimate success: "the gates of hell shall not prevail against it" (Matthew 16:18). Yet at the same time the Church is utterly human in that it consists of human beings who are not perfect. When its members have lived up to their calling, the Church has been dramatically successful in bringing God's love to men. When its members have been concerned only for their own comfort, the Church has been self-centered, corrupt, and irrelevant to the needs of society.

We think with horror of the Christians who silently assented to Hitler's extermination of the Jews, but also recall that the strongest force in opposition to Hitler was the confessing Church under the leadership of Dietrich Bonhoeffer, who was martyred by the Nazis in 1945. We think of the complacency of white suburbanite Christians toward racial inequality. But until recently nearly every black college in America was church-affiliated. And black and white people were brought together against racism by the apostle of Christian non-violence, the Rev. Martin Luther King, and his organization, The Southern Christian Leadership Conference.

The Church will recover its unity only when all Christian groups sit down together to rediscover Christ. The Church will truly and effectively be the Body of Christ when all Christians realize that they have but one purpose: to proclaim with their lives the one Christ to all mankind.

Prayer
and Sacraments

25

"Prayer. That's words said in church by a minister." Unfortunately this statement reflects all that prayer means to many people.

Prayer is natural. Men instinctively reach out, in the midst of the passing things of life, for what is lasting. Prayer is the lifting up of heart and mind to God. It is the avenue to God's presence. Prayer is a way of life. Jesus prayed constantly. He taught his disciples to do so in order that they might recall their lives to God's purpose: "Thy will be done." Prayer prevents us from becoming immersed in our own selfish concerns and worldly anxieties. When we pray we consciously put our lives at God's disposal so that he can act through us. Prayer is not magic: it is not the attempt to extort something from God. Prayer is not necessarily spoken; it does not necessarily take place in church. It is the instinctive offering of our whole being to God in the midst of life that we may be channels of his power and love. Prayer is the practice of the presence of God in our daily lives.

Prayer is the outgrowth of love. One cannot pray unless one really cares about oneself and others. One begins to learn to pray when one begins to learn to love. When we really care we begin to want things for others that we alone are unable to give them. Someone we love may be confused or sick or trapped by some destructive habit; we pray that God will touch his life and heal him, and we pray that our lives may be used for that purpose if God wants to act through us. Our parents or one of our children leave on a long automobile trip or to go to work. We cannot be physically present to help them, but we instinctively pray that they will be safe. And, of course, we look for opportunities to help those in whose lives we are physically present, hoping that others will help our absent loved ones. We observe mankind on the brink of self-destruction; we pray that our lives may not be given to hostility and anger, but rather be instruments of God's reconciling love.

Public Prayer

Jesus not only prayed alone in private; he prayed publicly. He taught his disciples to pray not "My Father" but *"Our* Father." It is natural for people with similar desires to join together to express their common concerns (about those who are sick, about injustice, about strife between nations). It is natural for a family to come together in their father's house to celebrate their kinship. Public prayer can, however, be fraudulent. The recital of beautiful old-fashioned words in church is not necessarily prayer. It may be a hypocritical parade of piety. Jesus spoke of the outward pious acts of the Pharisees: "Alas for you, lawyers and Pharisees, hypocrites! You are like tombs covered with whitewash; they look well from outside, but inside they are full of dead men's bones and all kinds of filth" (Matthew 23:27). Public prayer also has another danger. Since many participate in public worship it must be more formal than private prayer. Public prayer can, therefore, become a mere formality, the mindless, dry recital of familiar words. But prayer must be at least partly public. We are children of the same Father; we are a family. And private prayer alone can grow very narrow. When we come to church the concerns of others often remind us of things we would not otherwise be concerned about ourselves.

Prayer Is Always Answered

The heart of Christian prayer is expressed by Jesus in the Garden of Gethsemane as he is about to be arrested and crucified. He prays to God that "this cup [of death] may pass from me." But he concludes his prayer by asking: "Nevertheless, not *my* will but *thy* will be done." Some people say: "God doesn't answer prayer; he didn't do what I asked him." That view of prayer is utterly the opposite of Jesus' view. Jesus does not try to manipulate God, to force God to do what he wants him to do. Jesus' prayer includes his desire to avoid death, and yet it concludes always with the truest prayer: "*Thy* will be done."

Fortunately God often refuses what we desire. C. S. Lewis has written: "If an infinitely wise Being listens to the requests of finite and foolish creatures, of course he will sometimes grant and sometimes refuse them." God always answers prayer, though not always the way we want him to or expect him to. The one request God never refuses—the prayer Christ himself taught us to pray—is the prayer: "Thy will be done." St. Francis of Assisi prayed "Lord, make me an instrument of thy peace." That prayer is never refused.

Sacramental Worship

Public prayer or worship is fundamentally sacramental. In fact, all of life is sacramental. A sacrament is the outward, physical, concrete expression or sign of an inward feeling. All *words* are sacraments: they concretely and outwardly express what we feel "on the inside." If we *feel* love on the inside we can express our inward feeling to someone only by a sacrament: we might say the words "I love you," or we might shake hands (the joining of hands is the outward sacramental way we express friendship), or we might kiss (the physical joining of lips is the outward sacramental way we express love). So words and physical actions (like kisses, handshakes, and salutes) are all sacraments.

The Christian life is profoundly sacramental. First, Christians believe that the unseen spiritual God came to earth as a concrete visible man. Second, Christians believe that God conveys his love and power to us in concrete ways. God always loves us and his power is always present in our lives, but he expresses his love toward us on occasion, in time, in concrete acts; namely, the sacraments of his Church. God acts, thus, in much the same way as a parent to a child: a parent always loves a child and wishes to help him, but at times, perhaps when a child goes to bed, he expresses the love he always feels in a kiss, a concrete act at a definite time. So the sacraments are the outward signs, in time, by which God expresses his timeless love for us and conveys strength to us.

The Prayer Book defines a sacrament (pages 292 and 581) as "an outward and visible sign of an inward and spiritual grace given unto us; ordained by Christ himself, as a means whereby we receive this grace, and a pledge to assure us thereof."

"*A Sacrament is an outward and visible sign of an inward and spiritual grace.*" Outward things can become charged with significance and value, even though their physical appearance does not change. We can see a wedding ring in a jewelry store; we can say it is shapely or attractively set. Once the ring has been purchased and given, however, its significance is more than its appearance. Its value is more than its physical properties.

"*As a means whereby we receive this grace, and a pledge to assure us thereof.*" The Christian sacraments are not merely signs or symbols. They actually convey what they symbolize. A kiss is not just a sign or symbol of affection, it *conveys* the affection it symbolizes.

Two of the Church's sacraments, Baptism and Communion, were explicitly commanded by Christ. We call these two "Dominical" (which means "Our Lord's") or "greater sacraments." There are five other sacraments of the Church which we have no record of Christ explicitly commanding. Yet all five were practiced by his closest followers and we have every reason to think they are the carrying out of his desires.

The chart on the next two pages briefly outlines the Christian sacraments.

Sacrament	Outward Sign	Inward Grace	What We Do	Officiant
Holy Baptism (PB, 273)	Water, in the name of the Trinity.	Washing away of the old life, spiritual rebirth as God's child. Made members of Christ's body, the Church, with opportunity for growth.	Recognize evil and reject it. Believe in Christ's saving power. Pledge to try to act in line with our beliefs.	Bishop, Priest, or Deacon. Anyone in an emergency.
Confirmation (PB, 296)	Laying on of hands.	Strengthening by the Holy Spirit to take up, as adults, our full Christian responsibilities.	Renew commitment made at Baptism. Pledge discipleship to Christ.	Bishop only.
The Lord's Supper (Holy Eucharist, Mass, or Holy Communion) (PB, 67)	Bread and wine.	The real presence of Christ conveyed to us as we gather together at his command to recall to ourselves his life and teachings.	Prepare ourselves carefully: repent and resolve to "lead a new life."	Bishop or Priest.
Absolution (PB, 76, 323)	Sign of Cross with right hand.	God's forgiveness of our sins if we truly repent.	Repentance and true intention to amend our lives.	Bishop or Priest.

Sacrament	Outward Sign	Inward Grace	What We Do	Officiant
Matrimony (PB, 300)	Couple join hands and exchange rings. (Ring is a circle without ends, symbolizing lifelong commitment.)	God's blessing on the marriage, his grace to help the couple keep their promises.	Pledge to enter lifelong partnership that involves growth in self-giving and self-sacrifice.	Couple marries each other. Bishop, Priest, or Deacon blesses marriage.
Unction (PB, 320)	Laying on of hands or Anointing with holy oil.	God's healing power at work.	Express our need and faith.	Bishop or Priest, or layman administering oil blessed by Priest.
Holy Orders (PB, 530, 536, 549)	Laying on of hands.	Commissioning by Christ to a particular office (Bishop, Priest, or Deacon) in the Church.	If called, we seek academic and spiritual preparation.	Bishop only.

Baptism— 26
Sacrament of Belonging

The Christian life begins when man responds to God's initiative. God doesn't force himself on man; man must freely decide to accept or reject God. Yet in the eyes of many, the Church appears to try to force God on defenseless infants when it baptizes them before they can possibly know what is happening to them.

The reasons for infant Baptism will be dealt with later in detail. The important thing to note at this stage is that even when infants are baptized, a decision and commitment to respond to God in belief and in action is made by an adult *on the child's behalf.* In the case of adult Baptism, of course, the adult himself makes that decision and commitment on his own behalf. In *all cases,* therefore, except in an extreme emergency, an act of decision and commitment must *precede* Baptism.

Jesus spoke of two births—our physical birth and our spiritual birth. Our spiritual birth occurs when we awaken to God, respond to him. In most of us it is gradual, even unnoticeable, though in some it is sudden and dramatic. In some it never takes place at all. Jesus talks about it in his conversation with Nicodemus in John's Gospel. John undoubtedly means for us to regard Nicodemus' coming at *night* as more than literal.

There was one of the Pharisees named Nicodemus, a member of the Jewish Council, who came to Jesus by night. 'Rabbi,' he said, 'we know that you are a teacher sent by God; no one

could perform these signs of yours unless God were with him.'
Jesus answered, 'In truth, in very truth I tell you, unless a man
has been born over again he cannot see the kingdom of God.'
'But how is it possible', said Nicodemus, 'for a man to be born
when he is old? Can he enter his mother's womb a second time
and be born?' Jesus answered, 'In truth I tell you, no one can
enter the kingdom of God without being born from water and
spirit. Flesh can give birth only to flesh; it is spirit that gives
birth to spirit. You ought not to be astonished, then, when I
tell you that you must be born over again. The wind blows
where it wills; you hear the sound of it, but you do not know
where it comes from, or where it is going. So with everyone
who is born from spirit.'   JOHN 3:1-8

Remember that "wind" and "spirit" are the same word in
Greek. We cannot define how God's Spirit acts or where it
comes from, but it nonetheless affects men, giving them a
"new lease on life."

Sacrament of Rebirth

Baptism is the sacrament of rebirth. The person who
wishes to respond to God and to grow as God's child is made,
in Baptism, part of a community to grow as a child of God.
Being baptized is rather like enrolling in a university: we
wish to train our minds in a certain way, and we therefore
put ourselves in a situation in which, with hard work, we will
grow toward that goal, while outside that situation, obviously, our chances of growth are less. In Baptism a person
is enrolled in a community which seeks to respond to God,
and in which he can grow in insight. Thus Baptism does not
instantly transform people from bad to good. It alone, however, opens up to them a unique opportunity for growth, a
growth which is continuous, which, in fact, never ends in
earthly life.

Every group has its own way of admitting new members.
The Jews had long baptized gentile converts to their faith.

"To baptize" means "to wash" or "to cleanse." John the Baptizer, you recall, infuriated the respectable Jews by telling them they needed to "repent and be baptized." Jesus took over the Jewish custom of baptism and made it the outward symbol of spiritual birth. He told his disciples:

'Go forth therefore and make all nations my disciples; baptize men everywhere in the name of the Father and the Son and the Holy Spirit. And be assured, I am with you always, to the end of time.'   MATTHEW 28:19-20

The disciples, of course, carried out this command. In chapter 18 we read of Peter in his first address urging people to "repent [literally, turn your lives around] and be baptized." And we find Paul very soon exhorting some of those who have been baptized into the community to live up to the sort of life they embarked upon at their Baptism.

The Baptism of Infants

In the early Church, those who sought to be baptized were mainly adults. They heard the message, responded, sought rebirth to a new way of life, and were baptized. Yet, before long, whole families (including servants and children) were baptized when the head of the household was baptized. Thus it became common for persons to be baptized before they consciously had turned to God or expressed desire to be baptized. And since Baptism is not a magical rite, the Church early insisted that for those who had not yet reached the "age of discretion," "sponsors" (we call them "godparents") would have to express the intention to lead a new life and the desire to be baptized on behalf of the child, until he was old enough to express it himself.

Even though infant Baptism can easily be misunderstood as magical or as a quaint naming festival, the Church has practiced it from early times for good reason. Baptism gives a child the opportunity to grow up within the Christian community with the benefits of its care and education. Godparents specifically promise to see that the child learns what the Christian life is. Children learn values from their surroundings all through childhood: from parents, friends, school, comic books, television. It would be unnatural for Christian parents not to want their children to learn about the values Christ teaches and to grow up in the Christian community. We send a child to school without consulting his wishes in the matter. When he is older that child, if he wishes, can refuse to continue. Similarly when a child reaches "the age of discretion" he is given the opportunity to accept (at Confirmation) or reject the Christian way of life in which his parents launched him at Baptism.

The Baptismal Rite

a. WHAT WE DO IN BAPTISM

The first part of the baptismal service is the expression of desire to be reborn to a new way of life. Without that expression, and a commitment to try to grow as a follower of Christ, Baptism would be magical. Either we must make it for ourselves or, if we are infants or children, someone must make it for us until we are old enough to confirm it ourselves. The threefold act of repentance and commitment is found on pages 276 and 277 of the Prayer Book:

1. We promise first to *resist what is wrong:* "renounce the devil and all his works, the vain pomp and glory of the world, with all covetous desires of the same, and the sinful desires of the flesh." The devil is evil personified, all the instincts which we know will tempt us to anger, cruelty, selfishness, and thoughtlessness. We do not need to believe that evil is a person any more than we need to believe a ship is a person when we refer to it as "she." In rejecting evil we do not reject the world (which, as part of

God's creation, is good) but rather "the *vain pomp and glory* of the world," that is the love of money, possessions, and popularity. Likewise, we do not reject the desires of the flesh, but rather the "*sinful* desires of the flesh." When we enter an important athletic contest, we give up alcohol, smoking, and late nights to condition our body. Similarly if we wish to be in good condition spiritually, we will have to determine to resist temptations which make spiritual growth impossible.

2. We promise to *believe what is true:* "all the Articles of the Christian Faith, as contained in the Apostles' Creed." There have been people in every age who say "It doesn't matter what you believe as long as you're sincere." Christians, though they would admit that a racist or an anarchist, for example, is sincere, would nonetheless say he is wrong. Christianity is commitment to a definite way of life—growth in love as children of God.

3. The final commitment is to *do what is right:* "obediently keep God's holy will and commandments," to translate belief into action. For it is in our actions that the genuineness of our commitment is seen. Emerson wrote, "a man's life is a picture book of his creed."

b.   WHAT GOD DOES FOR US IN BAPTISM

In the early Church Baptism was often administered in a river. After his act of commitment, in a symbolic act, a person would take off his old clothes and enter the river. The priest would then immerse him three times in the water in the name of God—Father, Son, and Holy Spirit—and make the sign of the cross on his forehead. The newly baptized person would then emerge on the other side of the river and put on new white garments, symbol of the purity of his new life.

Though this is sometimes done today, usually a person is immersed in water or water is poured on his head. But the symbol of water still remains a powerful one. It symbolizes the *drowning* of our old life. Water is used for washing, symbolizing a cleansing from the past. Science shows us that water is the source of all life on earth—that all living things originally came from the water. The human embryo comes from the amniotic fluid which is practically the same as sea water. Water thus symbolizes new birth. Water quenches thirst and without it we would die: Christ satisfies all our longings and enables us truly to live.

The catechism states that in Baptism we are "made a member of Christ, the child of God, and an inheritor of the kingdom of heaven." This does not mean we instantly become perfect. It means that at Baptism these paths are opened to us, although our growth into them takes place over many years. Two twenty-year-olds get married. In one sense they are made one, but it really takes them years to grow more and more fully into a perfect oneness. Let us look then at what we become in Baptism:

1. *A member of Christ.* "Member" means "limb"; we are limbs of Christ's body, the Church. In our quest to become God's children we join ourselves to Christ, the perfect Son of God. Baptism is initiation into a community far larger than our class, our race, or our nation. It is initiation into the family of God of all ages—past and present—as brothers of Christ.

2. *The child of God.* Though we are potentially children of God at birth, in Baptism we accept our destiny as children of God and begin to grow as such. A person may have great intelligence but get bad grades in school because of laziness or lack of motivation. Then there comes a time, perhaps, when he says to himself, "I am intelligent and it's about time I did something about it and began to work."

He has now taken the first step and in school he will begin to accept the help his teachers have always tried to give. At Baptism we commit ourselves to become children of God. And God, who has always loved us as children, can now help us grow as his children.

3. *An inheritor of the kingdom of heaven.* We are not heirs; an heir is still waiting for his inheritance. We are inheritors; we have already begun in Baptism to live our lives in a wholly new and enlarged dimension as part of God's family.

The Unbaptized

Christ thought Baptism so important that he told his followers to go to the ends of the earth to baptize men. One indication of the importance with which the Church regards Baptism can be seen in the instructions on page 281 of the Prayer Book where it is shown how anyone (not necessarily a clergyman) may baptize an unbaptized person in an emergency.

But we must remember that God loves and guides men in many ways, fortunately not just through the sacraments of the Church. Christians believe that Christ established Baptism as the normal way to enter and grow in the knowledge of God, and as the normal means by which God receives us explicitly as his children. Obviously there are good people who are not baptized. There are people who have full happy lives with one lung, but this does not mean that two lungs are not desirable. There are fine, successful people who have had no formal education, yet we do not encourage people to drop out of school. We want children and adults to have every opportunity and advantage for growth. As Christians we believe the inclusion of persons in the Christian community is an advantage for them as they seek to discover the meaning and values of life.

Confirmation

27

In the early Church Baptism was almost always followed immediately by what we now call Confirmation. An apostle would lay his hands on the head of the newly baptized person and pray that the Holy Spirit would strengthen him as he took up the Christian life. After Philip, who was a deacon and not an apostle, had made and baptized converts to the faith, Acts tells us that the apostles Peter and John "prayed for them that they might receive the Holy Spirit; for it had not yet fallen on any of them, but they had only been baptized in the name of the Lord Jesus. Then they laid their hands on them and they received the Holy Spirit" (Acts 8:15-17, RSV). At Ephesus, after baptizing converts the apostle Paul "laid his hands on them, [and] the Holy Spirit came upon them" (Acts 19:6). The Letter to Hebrews refers to Confirmation as one of the "rudiments of Christianity" (Hebrews 6:1-2).

In the time of the apostles, therefore, Confirmation usually followed immediately after Baptism. It was administered only by the apostles. As the apostles died they passed their office and ministry as chief pastors on to their successors the bishops who were therefore authorized to confirm.

As the number of Christians increased, it became impossible for bishops to be present for the laying-on-of-hands immediately after every Baptism. Thus Baptism became separated from Confirmation. In the Eastern Church bishops allowed their priests to confirm with oil which the bishops had consecrated. But in the Western Church, bishops reserved for themselves alone the right to confirm. The custom grew up in the West, therefore, that children were baptized by their priest individually, at a convenient time, and were later confirmed in a group when the bishop was able to visit their parish. As part of the Western Catholic Church, the Anglican Communion follows this custom. Confirmation, the completion of Baptism, thus is usually separated by a number of years from Baptism.

Sacrament of Discipleship

In the Anglican Communion, Confirmation is administered only to those who "have reached the age of discretion," the age when they are able to think and to ask the important questions about the meaning of life. Baptism normally takes place in infancy, with sponsors making the commitment on behalf of the child. When the child becomes an adult he decides for himself whether to be a Christian and to complete his Baptism by being confirmed. He can only make such a decision after he has studied Christianity so that he understands what it is and is in a position to accept or reject it.

We know that, following Jewish custom, Jesus was circumcised and presented in the temple as an infant. But when we see him at age twelve, he is asking the important questions about the meaning and value of life. Naturally he asked these questions of the leaders of the religion in which he had been brought up.

Now it was the practice of his parents to go to Jerusalem every year for the Passover festival; and when he was twelve, they made the pilgrimage as usual. When the festive season was over and they started for home, the boy Jesus stayed behind in Jerusalem. His parents did not know of this; but thinking that he was with the party they journeyed on for a whole day, and only then did they begin looking for him among their friends and relations. As they could not find him they returned to Jerusalem to look for him; and after three days they found

him sitting in the temple surrounded by the teachers, listening
to them and putting questions; and all who heard him were
amazed at his intelligence and the answers he gave. His parents
were astonished to see him there, and his mother said to him,
'My son, why have you treated us like this? Your father and I
have been searching for you in great anxiety.' 'What made you
search?' he said. 'Did you not know that I was bound to be in
my Father's house?' But they did not understand what he
meant. Then he went back with them to Nazareth, and continued to be under their authority; his mother treasured up all
these things in her heart. As Jesus grew up he advanced in
wisdom and in favour with God and men.   LUKE 2:41-52

Parents are often bewildered and threatened by the questionings of their children, but there comes a time when every
individual must decide for himself the goals of his own life.
He must question the views of his parents; he must consider
the various alternative ways of life. And, finally, on his own
and for himself he must decide what he values and how he
wishes to live.

If he wishes to affirm for himself the Christian way of life,
he then can decide to be confirmed. Confirmation involves a
twofold commitment:

First (PB, 296), we renew on our own behalf the promises
we made or that were made for us at Baptism. These promises (discussed in the previous chapter) are threefold: to
try to recognize evil and resist it; to believe and trust in God;
to put our belief into action.

Second (PB, 297), we make the great commitment of discipleship: "to follow Jesus Christ as our Lord and Saviour."
This is the heart of Confirmation. On our own, as individuals,
we make a personal public commitment to follow Christ.

Sacrament of Strengthening

Thomas Aquinas, the medieval philosopher, wrote that
Confirmation is "the sacrament of strengthening, associated

with the increase of grace and with the arming of the Christian for spiritual warfare. As such it is the perfecting and completing of Baptism." After we have made our public commitment to Christ, the bishop leads the whole congregation in praying that we will be strengthened to live up to the commitment we have just made.

Then (PB, 297) the bishop lays his hands on our heads, saying "Defend, O Lord, this thy child with thy heavenly grace." The word "defend" comes from a Latin word meaning "strengthen." The bishop, by outwardly laying his hands on our head, expresses the prayer of the whole Christian community that we will be strengthened by God to have the courage to be faithful disciples. It is the bishop who lays his hands on our heads, rather than the local priest, both because that was the custom of the early Church, and because the bishop's presence emphasizes that we are not joining some local club, but are becoming consenting members of the worldwide community of Christ's followers.

Confirmation is the beginning of a lifelong growth as disciples. The bishop goes on to pray for each person "that he may continue thine for ever; and daily increase in thy Holy Spirit more and more, until he come unto thy everlasting kingdom."

Every confirmed Christian is a *minister*. Every confirmed Christian is called upon to follow Christ, to tell others of his teachings, and to demonstrate in his own life the love of Christ to everyone he encounters. The word "minister" means "servant"; and Confirmation is our commissioning or ordination as ministers. Paul wrote to the Corinthians: "It is not ourselves that we proclaim; we proclaim Christ Jesus as Lord, and ourselves as your servants, for Jesus' sake" (2 Corinthians 4:5).

Each individual has his own way of serving God. Paul writes that "men have different gifts, but it is the same Spirit who gives them. There are different ways of serving God, but it is the same God who achieves his purposes through them all. Each man is given his gift by the Spirit that he may use it for the common good" (1 Corinthians 12:4-7, Phillips). So Confirmation comes down to our giving our lives to God that he may act through them. St. Francis of Assisi perfectly expressed this in his great prayer:

O Lord, our Christ, may we have thy mind and thy spirit. Make us instruments of thy peace; where there is hatred, let us sow love; where there is injury, pardon; where there is discord, union; where there is doubt, faith; where there is despair, hope; where there is darkness, light; and where there is sadness, joy.

O divine Master, grant that we may not so much seek to be consoled as to console; to be understood, as to understand; to be loved, as to love; for it is in giving that we receive; it is in pardoning that we are pardoned; and it is in dying that we are born to eternal life. Amen.

The Lord's Supper–1

28

Baptism and Confirmation are the sacraments of initiation.
The Lord's Supper is the sacrament of continuation or re-
newal. An ancient word describing the Lord's Supper was
viaticum, meaning "food for the road." The Acts of the
Apostles tells us that the early Christians met from the beginning to break bread together in response to Jesus' request at
the Last Supper: "Do this in remembrance of me." Though
in the next few centuries controversies over doctrine and
practice often divided the Christian community, no one disputed the central importance of the Church gathering each
Sunday to celebrate the Lord's Supper.

The very name "The Lord's Supper" recalls to our minds
the last two days of Jesus' life. It is Thursday night. Judas
has betrayed Jesus. In a few hours he will be arrested and
hastily tried, and on Friday he will be executed. Starting
Friday night the Jews will celebrate, with a thanksgiving
dinner, the Passover Festival, the commemoration of the
passing over of the Jews to safety and freedom from their
enslavement in Egypt. Jesus celebrates the Passover with his
disciples a night early, on Thursday rather than Friday. In
place of the lamb (which at the festival is killed, offered to
God, and then eaten), Jesus puts himself. He takes two
simple fruits of the earth: wheat and grapes, bread and wine.
And he says of them: "This is my body and blood, my real
self, which I am conveying to you by means of bread and
wine. To remember me after I am gone, do this: break bread

and share the common cup." Jesus therefore gives his disciples a sacrament or sign by which to recall his presence.
Just as we convey our inward friendship to someone by the
outward sign of joining hands, or our love by joining lips,
Jesus says he will be present among his disciples as they
break bread and share the common cup.

Words, Customs, and Vestments

Christians over the years tried to find the right words and
actions to express themselves as they came together in response to Jesus' request: "Do this in remembrance of me."
The Christian community in each place developed its own
liturgy, or regular words and actions used to celebrate the
Lord's Supper. Naturally what was best in one place was not
necessarily best in another. Thus many liturgies were used
in the early Church. Likewise, many are used today. The
Episcopal Church has authorized a number of liturgies for
trial use and will probably eventually have several official
liturgies, each suitable for use in different circumstances. And
throughout the Anglican Communion there are at least forty
authorized liturgies for the Lord's Supper. Other com-
munions have a similar multiplicity. This situation serves to
remind us that it is the liturgy itself, and not the words in
which it is expressed, that is important.

There is a similar diversity of customs. Different com-
munions adopt different postures in their liturgies. Generally,
in Anglican tradition, the congregation stands for hymns
(psalms, canticles, the Creed), sits for instruction (lessons
and sermon), and kneels for individual devotion and prayers
of penitence. But, of course, it is the individual's inward
sincerity, and not his posture, that is important.

Certainly, in the same way, it is not important what those

attending and taking part in the service wear. However, many Roman Catholics, Anglicans, and Lutherans have thought it helpful for those in charge of the liturgy to wear vestments which are related to the life and death of Jesus. Therefore the vestments listed below are sometimes used as an aid to us in recalling the setting of the Last Supper.

Amice. This neck band or scarf was used originally for protection from the cold. It symbolizes the blindfold put over Christ's eyes when he was beaten by the soldiers as he was about to be crucified.

Alb. The alb is the long white linen garment that falls from the shoulders to the ground. The word "alb" comes from the Latin word meaning "white." The alb was the simple undergarment worn by all civilized persons in the Roman world. Its simplicity and the symbolic purity of its color make it particularly fitting for the priest who acts as God's servant. When he was arraigned before Herod, Jesus was stripped of all his clothes except his alb.

Girdle or *Cincture.* Around the waist goes this rope belt which serves an obvious purpose. It symbolizes the whip with which Jesus was beaten and the rope with which he was tied at his trial.

Maniple. This waiter's napkin placed on the forearm symbolizes that the priest is the servant of the congregation. It reminds us of the towel Jesus used to wipe the feet of his disciples shortly before he was arrested and crucified.

Stole. The long colored scarf worn around the neck is called a stole. Jesus and his disciples, following Jewish custom, undoubtedly used a garment like this for a prayer shawl. Going around the neck, the stole symbolizes the yoke of service which is the priest's calling: to serve the Lord's servants, to minister to the ministers. The stole symbolizes the heavy cross laid on Christ's shoulder as he walked to his crucifixion.

Chasuble. This poncholike garment was the common outer clothing of the ancient world. For a big celebration or party a person wore as beautiful a chasuble as he could afford, just as today we get dressed up on occasion. Jesus undoubtedly wore a chasuble at the Last Supper.

Choirs and acolytes wear vestments so that their own clothes are hidden. No one can know whether their clothes are threadbare or of the finest quality. The servants of God are equal.

While words, customs, and vestments may be helpful, we must always bear in mind that they are trivial in comparison with the actual coming together of the people of God in response to Jesus' command.

We will now look at one of the many liturgies for the Lord's Supper, namely that found in the Prayer Book of the Episcopal Church. Like most liturgies, it is divided into two parts. First, the proclamation of the word of God in prayer, song, readings from Scripture, and sermon. And second, our response of offering, thanksgiving, and communion. In this chapter we will deal with the first half of the liturgy, and in the next chapter with the other half.

The Liturgy of the Word

1. *The Preparation* (PB, 67) consists of confession and greeting. We prepare ourselves for every significant event in life: a football game, a party, a test, a business engagement. Similarly we prepare ourselves for the Lord's Supper. Upon entering the church we kneel and confess our shortcomings to God. We greet each other in the name of God and ask God to help us to approach him sincerely.

2. *Christ's Summary of the Law* (PB, 69). This golden rule of agape pinpoints in a sentence all that Christ lived and taught.

3. *Kyrie eleison* (PB, 70) is our response to Christ's summary of the law, in which we acknowledge our failure to follow his example and teaching. We sometimes say the words in Greek, the language of the early Christians, to show our solidarity with Christians of all ages, and as a reminder that the language of faith is not really translatable into any language.

4. *Gloria in excelsis* (PB, 84). Though the Prayer Book places this hymn at the end of the service, most liturgies place it here, and many Episcopal churches use it at this point. It seems an appropriate place in which to thank God for his love for us in spite of our failures. The Gloria probably grew out of the song of the shepherds who greeted Jesus' birth. In penitential seasons (Advent and Lent) this hymn is omitted or replaced by something more suitable for the season.

5. *The Propers* (PB, 70). A proper Collect, Epistle, and Gospel are appointed for each Sunday and a number of other days ("holy days") on which we celebrate the lives of saints or special events in the life of Christ. These "propers" can be found in PB, 90-269.

   a. *The Collect* collects together the various requests and petitions of the congregation into one prayer. The collect is therefore the week's collective prayer of all Christians on earth. It usually requests God's help to keep what is asked of us in the lesson, Epistle, or Gospel which follow.

   b. An *Old Testament Lesson* reminding us of God's love at work before Christ may sometimes be included here.

   c. *Epistle* means "letter." An Epistle is part of one of the New Testament letters.

   d. *The Gospel Procession* follows the Epistle. The Missal (the book containing the Liturgy and the Propers) is moved from the south to the north end of the altar, or is carried into the congregation. This procession symbolizes the spread of the news about Jesus through the whole world. In the early days, of course, the north was still unchristian and in need of conversion.

e. *Gospel* means "good news," and the Gospel at the Lord's Supper is a portion of one of the four Gospels.

6. *The Sermon* is an explanation of or elaboration on the collect, lesson, Epistle, or Gospel, in which God's word is directly related to our lives.

7. *The Nicene Creed* (PB, 71) summarizes the central events of the Bible's account of what God has done and is doing. In the Creed we remind ourselves of these events and express our commitment to God who is creator (Father), who came among us as a man in Jesus (Son), and who guides us today (Spirit).

8. *The Prayer of Intercession* (PB, 74-75). Though the Prayer Book places this after the Offertory (symbolizing the offering of our prayers to God), most revised liturgies place the prayer here. It seems the most natural place in which to respond to God's word, to ask him to use our lives as instruments of his love and peace. In many liturgies, this is a very loose prayer in which individuals in the congregation can insert requests of their own.

9. *The Peace.* Though the Prayer Book makes no provision for it, most liturgies have restored this custom of the ancient Church. The Jews exchanged the greeting "Shalom" (Peace) as a sign of their unity and brotherhood. The first words of the risen Christ to his disciples were "Peace be with you!" The early Christians celebrated their brotherhood with one another by echoing Christ's words, usually augmenting the words with some tangible sign, such as shaking hands or embracing.

10. *Confession* (and Absolution) (PB, 75) may occur at any one of a number of places in the first part of the service. In the confession we realistically face our failures and resolve to lead a new life.

The Lord's   *29*
Supper–2

The Liturgy of the Eucharist

Eucharist means thanksgiving. The Eucharist is our joyful response of offering, thanksgiving, and communion after we have heard the good news of God's continuing love for us. Prepared by confession, by the word of God, and by prayer, we now come to the Lord's Supper itself.

1. *The Offertory* (PB, 72-73). Our first responsive step is the offering of our lives to God. In one of the Church's new liturgies the minister invites the people this way:

Beloved in Christ, the Gospels tell us that on the first day of the week, the same day on which the Lord rose from the dead, he appeared to his disciples in the place where they were gathered, and was made known to them in the breaking of bread. Come then to the joyful feast of the Lord. Let us prepare his table with the offerings of our life and labor.

Occasionally you hear someone remark: "I don't go to church. I get more out of staying at home." Or more specifically: "I don't go to Communion because I don't get anything out of it." Such a person has Christianity (and the Lord's Supper) turned upside down. Jesus taught that the whole point of life is not to get but to give. If a person comes to the Lord's Supper to get something—a nice warm feeling, cheap love, or sentimental encouragement—he will never find it. The Lord's Supper begins with the offering of "our-

227

selves, our souls and bodies, to be a reasonable, holy, and living sacrifice" to God. Just to be present, to enjoy the music or the sermon or the liturgy, is not necessarily to offer ourselves. Truly to offer ourselves is to come with all our cares and concerns, joys and sorrows, our wealth of talents and successes, and our weaknesses and failures. Truly to offer is to lift up our entire lives to God, to give our lives to him so that he can refresh them for the journey of life and use them for his purpose.

At the Offertory we offer ourselves by means of symbols. We are the caretakers of God's world in the years we are on earth (what is ours was not always ours and will not always be ours). Therefore we offer back to God a portion of the material possessions he has given us to use, as a reminder that they are really his not ours, and that others less fortunate can benefit from them. The ushers bring to the altar not only our financial offering, but the bread and wine that will be used as well. This symbolizes our offering back to God the fruits of the earth—wheat and grapes. But money, bread, and wine are all symbols of our offering our lives to God.

2. *The Thanksgiving* (often called "the Consecration") (PB, 76-82). This is the heart of the liturgy. In a great outpouring of thanksgiving we offer our lives to God and they are given back to us consecrated, lifted up, transformed, renewed. The bread and wine we offer are now made the vehicles by which Christ conveys himself to us: "This is my Body, this is my Blood."

   a. *Sursum Corda* (PB, 76) in English means "Lift up your hearts." Now we lift ourselves above what is trivial and temporary to what is lasting, to give thanks for God's love and to rejoice at the meeting which is about to take place.

   b. In the *Sanctus* (PB, 77) we join with men of all ages and places, with angels and archangels and all the company of heaven, to offer thanks to God in the words of the prophet Isaiah (6:3). The angels are not here for decoration. We now lift ourselves up beyond the passing things of this world to the heavenly dimension they symbolize.

c. *The recalling of Christ's offering of his life on the cross, and of his command to remember him in breaking the bread* (PB, 80). Christ's life of perfect love is summarized by his sacrificial death. His words at the Last Supper are repeated because Christ "did institute, and . . . command us to continue, a perpetual memory of that his precious death and sacrifice, until his coming again." This is the way he chose to have us remember him.

d. *Oblation, Supplication, and Invocation* (PB, 80-81). We join our offering to Christ's sacrificial offering of himself on the cross. And we pray that God will accept our lives, giving them back to us restored and renewed to serve him. Finally we ask that Christ will be present among us as we follow his command to remember him in the breaking of bread, so that strengthened by being with him, we may serve him in the world.

e. *The Lord's Prayer* (PB, 82). Jesus himself summarized the whole thankful offering of our lives to God in the prayer he taught his disciples: "Thy will be done." We repeat it here as the climax of our offering of ourselves.

3. *The Communion* (PB, 82-84). "And when he had given thanks, he brake it, and gave it to his disciples." Having given thanks, we now break the bread and share the cup. This is our act of union with Christ, who tells us "This is my Body and my Blood," and with each other since we are all one in Christ.

a. *The Breaking of the Bread* is done in silence. It was as the disciples broke bread on the night of the Resurrection that Jesus came among them, and it was when the disciples on the road to Emmaus broke bread that they recognized Jesus. We recall Paul's words to the Corinthian Christians: "When we bless 'the cup of blessing', is it not a means of sharing in the blood of Christ? When we break the bread, is it not a means of sharing in the body of Christ? Because there is one loaf, we, many as we are, are one body; for it is one loaf of which we all partake." (I Corinthians 10:16-17).

b. *The Administration of the Sacrament.* Sometimes a hymn is sung here as we approach the table of the Lord. What we have offered—bread and wine—is now given back to us, as Christ promised, as "the spiritual food" of Christ's Body and Blood, his real self. We are made one with Christ, he becomes present in our lives and gives us himself as "food for the road," refreshment on the way.

c. *A Final Prayer* (PB, 83) thanks God for receiving our offering of ourselves and for refreshing us with his presence. We pray that he will go with us as we go to serve him in the world.

d. *The Dismissal* (PB, 84). The dismissal reminds us that we have come to the Lord's Supper in response to Christ, in order to be strengthened to go out into the world to love.

The Lord's Supper–3

The Lord's Supper is called by many names. No one name is adequate; each emphasizes an important aspect of the Lord's Supper. We may look at those names in two categories.

What We Do at the Lord's Supper

1. *"The Lord's Supper"* reminds us of the Last Supper when Jesus, about to die, broke bread and told his disciples, "Do this in remembrance of me." *The first thing we do then is to remember* what Jesus did and said. This is more than a sentimental reflection. It is rather a vivid remembrance of Christ in relation to ourselves now.

2. *"Holy Communion"* emphasizes that *we come together to give ourselves* as a living offering to God. Nothing more naturally expresses human togetherness than eating together. A family gathers at a meal. At special meals—Thanksgiving or Christmas dinner—a family sets aside for a time all that is wrong and broken and celebrates its unity. At the Lord's Supper the Christian family celebrates its communion or unity. We come together, as brothers with a common father, to celebrate, to give thanks, and to be refreshed and strengthened to serve all mankind. Jesus promised that "where two or three have met together in my name, I am there among them" (Matthew 18:20). Christ, the host and head of the family, gathers us, his brothers, with him at the table.

3. *"The Holy Sacrifice."* We come to the Lord's Supper to give back and lift up our lives to God. We join the offering of our own lives ("this our sacrifice of praise and thanksgiving") with Christ's offering of his life to God on the cross. Christ's whole life is summed up in his sacrificial death, which showed his complete living out of the prayer "Thy will be done." At the Lord's Supper we join the imperfect offering of our lives to Christ's perfect sacrifice and offering:

> And now, O Father, mindful of the love
> That bought us, once for all, on Calvary's tree,
> And having with us him that pleads above,
> We here present, we here spread forth to thee,
> That only offering perfect in thine eyes,
> *The one true, pure, immortal sacrifice.*
> Look, Father, look on his anointed face,
> And only look on us as found in him. (Hymn 189)

4. *"Eucharist"* is the Greek for thanksgiving, and Eucharist is the most common name Christians have used through the centuries for the Lord's Supper. Thanksgiving is our response to God's gifts to us. A young man gives flowers to a girl, but not until the girl responds with gratitude can the relationship between them develop. Thanks is more than a social virtue. It is joyful acceptance of someone's free gift. So we can have no real relationship with God until we consciously and joyfully accept his gifts to us and thank him. The Lord's Supper is our Eucharist, our response of thankfulness for the blessings of intelligence, possessions, opportunities, health, and all that God has bestowed upon us in our years on earth. And this thankfulness opens us to a deeper relationship with God.

What God Does in the Lord's Supper

1. In *"The Blessed Sacrament"* of bread and wine the real presence of Christ is conveyed to us. A handshake is not

merely a sign of friendship, but it conveys, by the joining
of hands at a definite time and place, our real inward friendship. So the consecrated bread and wine are not only signs
of his Body and Blood (flesh and blood are signs of a real
living presence), but convey Christ's living presence to us
at a definite time and place. A mother's love for her child
is continual, but at a definite time and place she expresses
that affection, which is always there, by a kiss—a physical
and concrete expression of her constant love. So God is
present everywhere in the world, and he expresses his constant presence at a definite time and place in the Lord's
Supper, the physical and concrete expression of his real
presence. In the Lord's Supper Christ gives us an appointed
meeting place where we may realize his constant presence
and "dwell in him and he in us." Since this is the place appointed for our meeting with Christ, and since the consecrated bread and wine represent his living presence and also
convey that presence, we usually receive the sacrament on
our knees.

God accepts the offering of our lives. The fruits of the
earth (wheat and grapes) which we have offered to God,
God now gives back to us as "the spiritual food of the Body
and Blood of Christ." Christ is made present in our lives. He
is the "bread of life," our "food for the road," our nourishment in the midst of life.

2. *"The Mass"* is a popular name for the Lord's Supper.
Mass comes from the Latin word for "depart" and reminds
us that we have come to the Lord's Supper to be strengthened in order that we may go out into the world to "do those
good works which God has prepared for us." We have been
refreshed not so that we "have a nice warm feeling" or so
that we will be relieved of our anxieties. We have come to
be refreshed and renewed to be better servants of our
brothers.

Appendix A:
The Creeds

"Creed" comes from the Latin word *credo*, "I believe." Consciously or unconsciously every man has some basic belief that makes sense of the world and gives his life meaning. Several magazines have run long series of articles on topics such as "What I believe and Why" in which well-known people have expressed their views of life. These beliefs often appear to be non-religious: "I believe in man" or "I believe life's rewards spring mainly from work." Several contributors have expressed their belief that the universe is absurd and then gone on to discuss their belief that human life can be meaningful in the face of an absurd universe. But none of the contributors has ever claimed that he could *prove* his view of the universe or of life. For when we deal with the significance or meaning of things, we enter the realm of informed *belief*.

Naturally men with similar views about something get together. Bertrand Russell at one point issued, in conjunction with others, "An Atheist's Creed," in which he laid out certain principles of honesty, toleration, and maturity as being basic beliefs of atheists. Christian creeds were written because a number of people came to believe that the key to the meaning of life is found in Jesus Christ.

The first Christian creeds were the statements of belief made by new converts when they were baptized. As time went on these statements were elaborated, often to combat ideas which the Christian community felt were misrepresen-

tations of Jesus. By the fourth century the Apostles' Creed
(PB, 15), the probable outgrowth of a creed first used at
Rome in A.D. 150, was in wide use. In chapter 21 we have
already observed the development of the so-called Nicene
Creed (PB, 71).

The thought patterns and imagery of one generation are
different from those of another. Observe the bewildered
grandmother as she hears her grandson say, "I bombed my
test today; it was a total zip." Bomb and zip will conjure up
a very different set of images in her mind than the grandson
intended to convey. A creed is naturally stated in the
imagery of the time in which it is written. We recognize that
the Apostles' and Nicene Creeds are expressed in the images
and thought forms of 1600 years ago, but we still use them
today as adequate statements of Christian belief, remember-
ing the need to translate in our minds the images of the
fourth century into those of the twentieth.

Some people ask why creeds are necessary at all. First,
necessary or not, it is natural for people who agree about
something important to celebrate their agreement. But the
creeds serve another useful purpose. As individuals our
tendency is to take certain aspects of Christianity (perhaps
what we find most congenial) to the exclusion of other
aspects. The creeds constantly present us with what the
Christian community through the ages has seen to be the full
richness of the faith. The creeds therefore help to keep our
personal faith from becoming narrow and perverted.

Let us look now at the phrases of the Nicene Creed.

God the Father

I believe in God the Father Almighty. J. B. Phillips, in his
book *Your God Is Too Small,* talks of man's inadequate pictures of God: God as a grand old man who was once very
active in the world but who has now retired to heaven; God

as the voice of conscience (even though we know that conscience can be manipulated by society, as in Nazi Germany); God as the eternal negative, casting prohibitions everywhere and trying to eliminate all pleasure and happiness.

God is far beyond our full understanding. Since we are one of four billion little specks on a speck in the universe, we can hope for little more than glimpses and indications of the ultimate reality and meaning of things.

The Creed begins with the affirmation that the ultimate reality is God—that in relation to him we discover the meaning of life. The Creed's opening words are not "I believe *that*" but rather "I believe *in* one God" who is called "Father Almighty." God is not just the abstract principle of unity, or sheer Force or Mind. God is *personal*. Though he must be much more than personal and infinitely more than our imaginations can conceive, we can know him and be known by him. And we can trust him as a child trusts his father.

Maker of heaven and earth, And of all things visible and invisible. One question which confronts every person is whether the universe is purposeful and meaningful or absurd and meaningless. Atheists assert that the universe came into being by chance and that it is devoid of meaning. (See Bertrand Russell, *Why I Am Not a Christian.*) Christianity asserts that a non-material spiritual Force (who is personal) brought into being the first two proto-molecules which, speaking crudely, were rubbed together to start the whole process out of which developed the material universe, and that that Force or Mind gives to that universe both order and significance.

God the Son

And in One Lord Jesus Christ. Nothing is clearer from the Gospels than that Jesus was a human being like us: he was born, tempted, suffered, and died. Yet it is equally clear that

Jesus' life was so perfectly attuned to the Father that God's love and power flowed through it and that, in St. John's concept, he who has seen Jesus has seen God. In Jesus we see, in a human being, what God is like. As the perfect human disclosure of God we call Jesus divine.

The creeds therefore affirm both the complete humanity and the complete divinity of the single person Jesus Christ. Of the clauses which follow, the first four emphasize Jesus' divinity, the remainder his humanity:

The only-begotten Son of God; Begotten of his Father before all worlds. In chapter 2 we discussed God's progressive expression of himself in creation, nature, and the minds of man. Christ is not part of God's creation, but God's very expression of himself through whom all creation took place. As a son reflects his father, so, in Paul's words, Jesus "is the image of the invisible God" (Colossians 1:15). Christ is not created, he is begotten or generated from the being of God before all creation. He is God flowing out of God.

God of God, Light of Light, Very God of very God. The word "of" means "from" or "out of." Christ is God coming out of God, Light coming from Light, the True God out of the True God. Jesus' human life shows us God. St. Hippolytus remarks: "When I speak of the Son as distinct from the Father I do not speak of two Gods, but, as it were, light from light, the stream from the fountain, the ray from the sun."

Being of One Substance with the Father. This clause, we saw in chapter 21, was inserted specifically to combat the heresy of Arius. (Arius said that Jesus was *like* God, but was not God, but rather was a part of God's creation.) If Jesus was only an especially good man or someone strangely like God, then God has not really involved himself in our world or lived and suffered with us as one of us. Christ is God's Word, his expression of himself in human terms. Just as my words are "me" in that they convey me to you, so Christ is God in that he conveys God to us.

By whom all things were made. Christ, as God's expression of himself, is not among the created things that are "made," but he is the *means* by which God made all things. Christ is thus not part of the creation, but, as God's expression of himself, he is the means by which all creation took place.

Who for us men and for our salvation came down from heaven. This does not mean that heaven is a geographical place up in the sky from which Jesus literally descended. It expresses, in symbolic language, the fact that God did not remain aloof from his creation, but, in Christ, laid aside his divine privileges to be born, tempted, and to suffer and die as a man. Carroll Simcox remarks: "Ours is not a religion of man seeking God, it is a religion of God seeking man." (See chapter 2.)

And was incarnate . . . And was made man. To Christians this is the central event of all history. It is the affirmation that the God who has revealed himself in creation, in the minds of great men of all ages, finally expressed himself completely in a human being in history. (See chapter 2.)

By the Holy Ghost of the Virgin Mary. This phrase's main point is that God became a man at a definite time and place and was born of a very human mother. Chapter 3 contains a discussion of the significance of the word "virgin." Matthew alone (of all the writers in the New Testament) asserts that Jesus was born of a virgin. Though the other writers are silent, either because they did not know about such a theory or because they did not think it was important, they are all in agreement with Matthew in believing that in this human birth God entered into the world as a man. *That* God became a man is far more important than *how* God became a man.

And was crucified also for us under Pontius Pilate. He suffered and was buried. When God became human he went the whole way. He was born a man, suffered hunger, thirst, rejection by his friends, hideous pain, and finally death itself. The Creed jumps right from the birth of Christ to his death because his suffering and death summarize his whole life of self-sacrifice and love. The name of Pontius Pilate is recorded not that we should forever recall his role in the whole affair; it is here only to indicate that Christ's suffering and death were real and occurred at a definite time. (See chapter 15.)

He descended into Hell (from the Apostles' Creed). The word "Hell" translates two Greek words: *Hades,* the place where all departed spirits go at death, waiting in custody, as it were, for trial; and *Gehenna,* which means the place of punishment or damnation, the experience of separation from God. Hades is the word used here. This phrase affirms that Christ tasted death in all its depth and fullness, so that he is familiar with and subject to all of human experience from life to death and beyond.

And the third day he rose again. Jesus died. His disciples and friends deserted him in utter despair. He on whom they had pinned all hopes, for whom they had given up so much, had been murdered. Evil had triumphed over good. God had apparently rejected the man who had given his life totally to God. Three days later, however, we find this motley crew assembled together, changed completely. Now they felt Jesus was alive. Now they were willing to risk all, even life itself, to proclaim Christ. Some great event has to account for the transformation of the disciples. We call that event the Resurrection: the Jesus whom men put to death has overcome death, is alive, active in our lives. (See chapters 16 and 17.)

According to the Scriptures. Jesus was raised from the dead and was alive, fulfilling all that had been predicted and anticipated in the *Old* Testament Scriptures. (The Scriptures referred to are not, as is often thought, the New Testament accounts of Christ's resurrection.) The Incarnation (climaxed in the Resurrection) was not a sudden interruption of God's purpose, but the fulfillment and high point of his gradual revelation of himself.

And ascended into Heaven. The primary evidence for the Resurrection is the conviction of the disciples that Christ was alive. They felt his presence vividly for a period after the Resurrection, and then this visible presence ended. The Ascension is the pictorial description of the ending of this visible presence of Christ, and symbolizes two things. First, it signifies the end of Christ's vivid earthly presence and his return to the Father, restored to the state in which he was before the Incarnation. And second, it signifies the fulfillment by Christ of humanity's true end: to live and reign with God. (See chapter 17).

And sitteth at the right hand of the Father. Again we have a symbolic statement that Christ, after his Ascension, took back all those powers and attributes which he had laid aside when he came among us as a man. To sit on the king's right in ancient times was to occupy the place of highest honor. This clause also proclaims that Christ's victory, his triumph over evil, is permanent and eternal. "Right is on the throne." (See chapter 17)

And He shall come again, with glory, to judge both the quick and the dead. It is obvious that human life on earth is not always just: the good are often defeated and the evil prosper. This clause asserts, however, that there is an ultimate justice and that it is Christ who in the end is judge both of the living (which is what "quick" means) and the dead. We do not know what Christ's judgment will be like or when it will be. But we do assert two convictions: we are ultimately responsible to him for our lives, and we believe that ultimately, through him, the injustices of earthly life will be put right. Christ, as a man, knows our human frailties as well as our strengths. Christ, as God, judges with absolute fairness and justice. (See chapter 17.)

Whose kingdom shall have no end. Physical kingdoms and human empires of wealth or of possessions pass away. Through the ages, men have sought—in the midst of their transitory human lives—for what is truly lasting. And in the midst of the passing things of life men occasionally find themselves lifted out of themselves and of their world, into an experience of beauty and happiness and fulfillment, to glimpse what is lasting and real. Wordsworth described this as being "surprised by joy." This clause reminds us that though earthly things pass away, God's reign is eternal.

God the Holy Spirit

And I believe in the Holy Ghost. God disclosed himself first in creation, then in the minds of men, and finally, when men were ready, fully and completely in a single human being, Jesus of Nazareth. Yet God did not stop revealing himself to mankind or showing men his love after Jesus' earthly life. Jesus promised his disciples that after he departed from them God's Spirit would guide and strengthen them. Chapter 18 describes the experience of the disciples at Pentecost, when as promised they were given a new awareness of God's Spirit.

The words "Holy Spirit" attempt to describe God as he acts now in the present in our lives. The Greek word for Spirit or Ghost also means wind or breath.

God's action is like the *wind.* We cannot see the wind itself; we can see only the effects wind has: pushing back a leaf on a tree, or blowing a piece of paper along the street. We cannot see God, but we can see and feel his effects on our lives and the lives of others: his bending people's lives as leaves, his pushing of a person along the road of life.

God's action is like *breath*, which gives life to our bodies. When we are short of breath our energies and powers are diminished; when we are without breath we are dead. Breath is life itself. One who has breath is inspired (inbreathed). The breath of God transforms a physical body into a living personality. He is "the giver of life."

God's action in our lives is like the *spirit* (which, though unseen, is real) that pervades a winning team, and enthuses or inspires its members to higher attainment.

The Lord, and Giver of Life, Who proceedeth from the Father and the Son; Who with the Father and the Son together is worshipped and glorified; Who spake by the Prophets. Wind, breath, spirit, all describe the way God acts. Since God is the one who so acts, the action is not just blind impersonal force, but personal. We call the Spirit "Lord" along with the Father and Son. "Lord" is the name used to describe God in the Old Testament. We say the Spirit "proceeds from the Father and the Son" when we think in human terms and see God acting chronologically. We tend to think of him first as creator (Father), then as redeemer or revealer (Son), and finally as present source of life and strength (Spirit). Yet the Spirit of God who "spoke through the prophets" has inspired men's minds in all ages.

The Church

And I believe one, holy, Catholic and Apostolic Church. When Jesus departed from this earth he did not leave behind a book or a system of theology. He left a community. Jesus charged this community to continue what he had begun in his own lifetime—to bring to men God's love and power and purpose. Before he departed he promised that this community would be guided by his Spirit, inspired by his breath of life. Sometimes Jesus referred to the Spirit as "Paraclete" which means "Strengthener." Thus, though God is not limited to working only through the Church, it is a normal means by which God carries on the work of Christ. The Creed describes the Church in four ways.

The Church is one because it is the extension of Christ's life on earth. The Church is sometimes called the Body of Christ. Christ is one and we are united with him and with each other as parts of his body. And yet there are hundreds of different churches. We might liken the Church's present divided condition to a family in which the children of the same mother and father grow up, quarrel, and act as if they were members of different families. Though they *are* members of one family, and nothing can take away their blood relationship, they are nonetheless divided by their differences. The great Japanese Christian, Kagawa, once said, "I speak English very badly, and when I say 'denomination' some people think I am saying 'damnation.' I am not surprised. To me they are very much the same thing."

The Church is holy because it is the extension of Christ's life on earth, and because he promised that the Holy Spirit would guide and strengthen it. Obviously, however, since the Church is made up of people, it is not perfect, and its members often fail to give their lives fully to God. A boy may be intelligent and yet, for some reason, not get good grades. Hopefully he will eventually realize his potential and "become what he is." In a similar way, the Church must realize its holiness.

The Church is Catholic (which means universal) because it is not for certain races or classes, but for all men, in all places, at all times. It is the universal all-inclusive fellowship in which all men may realize their common brotherhood as God's children.

The Church is Apostolic because it is not a new and different thing in every country or every century: it traces its beginning to Christ's apostles, is presided over by their successors, and believes what they believed. Though a person as he grows and matures changes somewhat in outward appearance, he remains the same individual. Though the Church changes in certain respects in every place and age, it remains essentially the same. (See chapter 24.)

The Communion of Saints (from the Apostles' Creed). In th New Testament, the word "saint" (which comes from the Latin word *sanctus,* holy) describes *all* Christians. As time went on, however, the word came to be used to describe *distinguished* Christians. But the "Communion of Saints" really consists of Christians of all ages and places: not only the great and lesser Christians long dead, but also those alive on earth today. It is the whole Church, living and dead. In the timeless Body of Christ we share with Christians of all ages a common faith.

I acknowledge one Baptism for the remission of sins. Baptism is our initiation into the community of the Church. No matter how flagrantly we disobey the rules of the organization, no matter if we leave it altogether for a time, we can be initiated into it only once. (See chapter 26.)

And I look for the Resurrection of the dead: And the Life of the world to come. We believe that God's purpose for us is not limited to the few years in which we are on earth. We believe that after our physical bodies die we have the wholeness of life restored to us. The Apostles' Creed calls this the "resurrection of the body": this does not mean the physical body, but body in the sense of the whole person. We thus believe that our whole personality will be given opportunity after our death on earth "to continue to grow in thy love and service."

The Trinity

Though the concept of the Trinity is not mentioned by name in the creeds, it is implicit in them, and as such merits our attention.

Our earth is only a billionth of the vast universe, our planet only one of millions. Obviously the Mind or Purpose or Force behind the universe—God—is far beyond our understanding, far beyond the realm of physical existence in which we live, far beyond our limitations of time and change.

Though, as St. John declares, "no man has ever seen God," we believe that God has revealed enough of himself for us to know and understand him at our own level. We first see him in all things and beings around us—in nature and in other men, as a carpenter is reflected in a piece of furniture he makes. Here we call God "Father" or "Creator." Then we see God's power and love and purpose for us revealed in a man—Jesus Christ. Here we call God "Son" or "Redeemer" or "Saviour." Finally we feel God active in our lives. Here we call God "Spirit" because that describes the way he acts in our lives today.

Men are always trying to put God in a box and make him small enough to control. The Trinity is the best way we have found to describe God, without limiting either his being or his action.

When we say "God in three Persons," we do not mean by "person" an individual. Person, in Latin, means something like "aspect" or "role." Though God is one, we experience him principally in three ways, we view him from three aspects. We often see a human being from a different point of view than others see him. We know a man as our employer, perhaps, while others know the same man as a son or as a husband. Our description of him will be different from the other two, although he remains the same man. The single substance water is seen in three different "persons": as liquid, ice, or steam—yet it remains water.

Appendix B:
The Seasons of the
Church Year

Season	Meaning	Symbol	Color
ADVENT. 4 Sundays: late November to December 24. Penitential season.	The expectation of Jesus' coming (the Old Testament prophets and John the Baptist).	Alpha and Omega (first and last letters of Greek alphabet): Christ the beginning and the ending.	Violet, the subdued color, symbol of fasting and penitence.
CHRISTMAS. December 25 to January 5.	The Incarnation. Birth of Christ.	I.H.S., the first 3 letters of Jesus' name in Greek.	White, symbol of purity, joy, light, victory.
EPIPHANY. 2 to 6 Sundays after January 6.	Christ shown to the whole world. Visit of wise men. Baptism. Miracles.	The Star, like that which led the wise men to the baby Jesus.	White for Feast of Epiphany and Octave; then green.
PRE-LENT. (Septuagesima, Sexagesima, Quinquagesima: about 70, 60, 50 days before Easter.)	Preparation for the coming of Lent: Jesus' teaching on discipleship.	Heart: We prepare our hearts for the coming of Lent.	Violet

Season	Meaning	Symbol	Color
LENT. 40 days from Ash Wednesday to Saturday in Holy Week. Penitential season.	Jesus' 40-day ordeal in the wilderness. We look at our lives, undergoing similar self-examination.	The Cross: The symbol of sacrifice and of Christ's final obedience to the Father.	Violet
PASSIONTIDE. The period in Lent from Passion Sunday to Easter, including Palm Sunday, Maundy Thursday, Good Friday.	The Passion (suffering) and death of Jesus.	The Crown of Thorns placed upon Jesus' head by the mocking soldiers.	Violet (White for Maundy Thursday, black for Good Friday.)
EASTER. 40 days from Easter Day to the Ascension.	Christ's resurrection. His triumph over death.	Lily or circle which signify eternal life.	White
ASCENSION. 10 days from Ascension Day to Whitsunday.	The end of Jesus' resurrection appearances to the disciples. His ascension.	The Crown: Representing Christ the King, reigning over the universe.	White
WHITSUNDAY, usually called Pentecost, which means fiftieth. It comes 50 days after Easter.	Fulfillment of Christ's promise that the Holy Spirit will guide his disciples. Birthday of the Church.	The Dove: Representing the Holy Spirit. Tongues of fire.	Red, symbol of the fiery zeal of the Spirit-filled disciples.
TRINITY. About half the year, from the Sunday after Pentecost until Advent.	God as Creator (Father), Redeemer (Son) and present guide (Spirit). Jesus' teachings emphasized.	Triangle, symbol of the Trinity: one figure with three sides.	Green, the color of nature, symbolizing God's rule over all creation.

Appendix C:
Index of
Biblical Passages

(P before a reference indicates that though the biblical passage is not in the Prayer Book, its parallel from another Gospel is.)